# THE VAUXHALL AND BEDFORD STORY

# THE VAUXHALL AND BEDFORD STORY

*A Pictorial History of
Vauxhall Factory,
Cars and Bedford Commercial Vehicles*

Richard Hart

Farnon Books

Typeset by GCS, Leighton Buzzard
Printed by Biddles Ltd., Guildford

ISBN: 0 9511698 3 1

# Foreword

Thank you for sending a copy of your book *The Vauxhall and Bedford Story*. It makes most interesting reading.

It is full of interesting facts and provides a nostalgic trip down memory lane. You have obviously spent a great deal of time researching the details.

We greatly admire your efforts. Thank you for letting us see it and we wish you every success with publication.


BRYAN MILLIN
Chief Press Officer,
Corporate Affairs,
Vauxhall Motors Limited

# Contents

# Acknowledgements

I would like to thank those who, over the years, have supplied me with information or advice. In particular I would like to thank the following people for their help: Stephen Bunker, Miriam Carroll, N. J. Gray, Ron Hall, David Hillier, Tom Lawson, Tony Lines, Nigel Lutt, John Neumuller, David Stroud, Brian and Sheila Uridge, Jane Weeks and Bernard Wilks.

In addition I wish to thank the following organisations and individuals for allowing copies to be made from original photographs or for supplying prints: Bedford Record Office, The Chamber of Commerce & Industry for Bedfordshire and District, Gillian Davis, Beryl Hyde, Luton Museum and Art Gallery, *Luton News,* John Shorthouse, and Vauxhall Motors.

Finally in researching this book I have drawn on material published in the following books:

*Vauxhall - The Post-War Years,* Trevor Alder, Haynes Publishing Group, 1991.
*A Souvenir of Vauxhall,* Vauxhall Motors Ltd, 1935.
*A History of Vauxhall,* Public Relations Department, Vauxhall Motors Ltd, 1980.
*The Griffin Story,* Public Affairs Department, Vauxhall Motors Ltd, 1990.
*The Story of Vauxhall,* L. C. Darbyshire, Vauxhall Motors Ltd, 1946.
*The Vauxhall,* Peter Hull, Shire Publications Ltd, 1992.
*The Motor Men,* Peter King, Quiller Press, 1989.
*An Account of our Stewardship,* W. J. Seymour, Vauxhall Motors Ltd.
*Making of the Motor Car,* M. E. Ware, Moorland Publishing Company, 1976.

## Picture Sources

All the pictures have been supplied by Vauxhall Motors Limited with the exception of those listed below.

Bedford Record Office 13b, 24tb, 25t, 64t, 117t, 133b

Gillian Davis 65t

Richard Hart 35t, 45b, 46tb, 97tb, 101, 102tb, 112b, 113, 134t, 135t, 137tb, 138b

Beryl Hyde 57, 75tb, 76tb

Tom Lawson 126t

*Leighton Buzzard Observer* 109b, 127t

Luton Museum and Art Gallery 25b, 42b, 72b, 73t, 77tb, 78tb, 79b, 80tb, 81tb, 82t, 86b, 87tb, 88tb, 89b, 90t, 135b

*Luton News* 27b, 98b

John Neumuller 105

Lex Vauxhall 100tb, 136b

John Shorthouse 68b

The Chamber of Commerce & Industry for Bedfordshire and District 20t

# The Early Days

The origins of what became Vauxhall Motors can be traced to Wandsworth Road, London, SW8, where in 1857 the firm of Alexander Wilson & Company was founded to manufacture steam engines, pumps and refrigeration plant. By 1892 a limited company had been formed. Wilson was a far better engineer than businessman and it was not therefore surprising that the company found itself in financial difficulties. Wilson resigned and set himself up as a consultant engineer. A receiver was appointed in 1896 and in 1897 the firm was renamed the Vauxhall Iron Works Company Limited.

The name Vauxhall is derived from one Fulk le Breant (also spelt Falkes or Fulkes). Through marriage, he acquired his wife's house on the south bank of the Thames. This came to be known as Fulk's Hall – corrupted over the years to Fawke's Hall, later to Foxhall and eventually to Vauxhall. The name Vauxhall survived as a district of London; the famous Vauxhall pleasure gardens were created in the 17th century near the site of the original Fulk's Hall. It was near this spot that the Vauxhall Iron Works produced its first car in 1903.

The person credited with the creation of the first Vauxhall is F. W. Hodges, who served his apprenticeship with Alexander Wilson & Company as a marine engineer. A car, which was probably a Canstatt-Daimler, was bought and studied. Two experimental belt-driven cars were made. In 1902 Hodges, in association with J. H. Chambers, who was on the board, began work on the design of the first Vauxhall car. It made its appearance in 1903 at £136. It had a 989 cc horizontal single-cylinder engine, tiller steering, single chain drive and two-speed gearbox with no reverse.

The early Vauxhall cars were very well received. One customer said of his 1904:

"The average cost has worked out at one third of the upkeep of my horse . . . an inexpensive, reliable and comfortable means of locomotion say I."

In March 1905 a *Luton News* reporter paid a visit to the newly-arrived Vauxhall Iron Works establishment in Kimpton Road. This is what that reporter wrote:

‘. . . . the new works are set back some distance from the road and opening the main door, I found myself in a corridor leading to the various offices and was quickly shown into the Works Manager's room – a cosy little office, heated and lighted by electricity, and commanding a view of the whole of the extensive workshops. Mr A. E. Ash gave me a very cordial greeting and immediately put himself at my disposal.

## Established over 50 years

To get a little history of the firm was my first object and in the course of conversation I gathered that the firm which is just removing to Luton from the Wandsworth Road, London, has been established over 50 years, and until comparatively recent date was almost entirely engaged in marine engineering and pump work. From a small commencement at Vauxhall in premises which were originally a brewery, the firm has steadily increased until a change of quarters was practically forced upon them for lack of accommodation. Additional land had been built upon and all available room utilized when at last a move was decided upon, the work was being done on four storeys, the stores and engine room being in the basement and the pattern at the top of the buildings.

It was in June 1903 that the firm turned their attention to motor work, and the success attending this department quickly rendered it absolutely necessary for them to look about for larger and better equipped works. The auxiliary premises which were taken in close proximity to the Wandsworth Road Works were soon too small, in addition to which the need for concentration under one roof was recognised. Accordingly the firm cast their eyes on Luton – the advantages of which had been quite accidentally brought before them – and in due time they decided to acquire the six-and-a-half acres upon a portion of which their new works are erected. Their first production in the way of cars to bring them into prominence in the motor world was a right little car known as the Vauxhall five horse. From this they have developed to more pretentious things, and now they make nothing less than cars of the three cylinder type, and employ from 160 to 200 hands, according to pressure of work.

To a question on the difficulties of removal and an expression of surprise that they had already got so large a number at work – a glance through the window into the shop revealing a little army of workmen and plenty of machinery in full running – Mr Ash observed that they had then about 140 hands on at Luton and were gradually increasing the number week by week as the machinery was transferred from London. The process of removal had been going on in this way for some time, thus obviating any break in the output.

Chatting on business in this way, I gathered from Mr Ash that with their settlement in Luton it is the intention of the firm, in connection with the marine department to go in for motor launches, and to their motor car branch to add the delivery van business.

## Young Men at the Head

Mr Ash proceeded to conduct me through the building. Incidentally, my conductor informed me that Mr Hodges is the designer of the Vauxhall car and the head of the designing and drawing offices and I gathered that the directors of this progressive firm are mostly young men and enthusiastic in their work. Mr Ash whose special department is marine engineering, is himself well on the youthful side. He came to the firm as works manager in 1897 and joined the board two years later.

Passing into the workshop, the workmen's mess-room occupies the available space between the foreman's office and the drawing office and immediately next to the corridor. It has already been found too small, but the pressure is expected to be relieved when the workmen's cottages near at hand are occupied. A large gas cooker is provided for the use of the men.

Turning into the works at last, I found it a regular hive of industry. The building is divided into four main bays, each of 35ft span and each served with a traveller from end to end, the cranes ranging in size from one to twelve tons. Two of the bays are devoted to the marine engineering and the two on the left when entering the building from Kimpton Road are set apart from motor work.

## Electricity and Gas

The machinery are motor-driven throughout, Mr Cooke the Borough Electrical Engineer having convinced the directors of the very definite advantages of electricity over gas for power. In this connection Mr Ash spoke very highly of Mr Cooke's services. The Borough Electrical Engineer had made himself invaluable to them, nothing had been too much trouble for him to elucidate if his advice had been sought. It is gratifying to hear such testimony of a public official, and it is service of this kind which will spell success for the town's electrical undertaking. Six motors totalling 16 horse power are already in use and another of 17 horse power is being installed.

Whilst the offices are lighted and heated by electricity, the Lucas incandescent gas lamps have been utilised in the works, and the effect, Mr Ash told me, was splendid. There are also portable gas jets and tubes for each machine. The heating is by Musgrave's patent stoves.

## The Marine Department

Walking through the marine department, I learned that the firm construct engines up to a thousand horse-power and are contractors to the Board of Trade and Admiralty, the War Office, India Office, the Crown Agents for the Colonies, etc. A large amount of their trade is export to the Colonies and abroad. Just at the present moment they have not a great deal of marine work on hand, but they have over 50 motor cars, already sold, in course of making. They have just booked the machinery for two large stern-wheel steamers for the Egyptian Government.

At the railway end of the building stands the smithy with three fires from which the smoke is exhausted by fan, and there are two power hammers. Adjacent in the dispatching corner of the works, which is in the bay adjoining the railway siding are a testing plate and a testing tank.

## Motor Department

The machinery used in the motor department is naturally of a lighter type than that in the marine portion and amongst the tools we noticed boring mills, a Brown and Sharp gearcutter and Herbert's and other torret machinery for rapid reproduction of parts.

I observed that Brown and Sharp's gearcutter was an American machine, though one could not but admire its mechanism and beautiful finish. Mr Ash remarked that it was the standard gearcutter of the world and this led on to other conversation, from which I gathered that Vauxhall people are intensely patriotic and pride themselves upon every part of the Vauxhall car being British made; indeed they make every part of it themselves, except the tyres and the bodies, and as a matter of fact, the bodies may be claimed to be made locally, as the firm work hand in hand with Messrs Morgan and Co, of London and Leighton Buzzard, in this respect. In the course of further chat, Mr Ash explained to me the various stages of manufacture of a three throw crank shaft from the rough forging to the brightly finished article.

I was next shown a large number of aluminium gear boxes and crank cases, which must have represented a considerable sum of money when one remembers that the material costs something like half-a-crown a pound. Passing by the benches set aside for the fitting up of the gear boxes and for carburettors, we next discussed the Vauxhall clutch which is a feature of the car which this firm manufactures. Its principle is to get an easy taking up of the work of the motor. There are four leather faced discs which bear on the flat of the fly wheel under spring pressure before the main cone comes into operation and the result is a perfectly easy gliding of motion for the car.

Passing next to the frame department, I was able to watch the frames being mounted with springs, axles and wheels after which they are passed on to the erectors for fitting-in of the machinery. Then, as the cars are completed, they will pass through the doorway of the main building to the running shed or garage.

## Workmen's Dwellings

The site acquired by the Vauxhall Company is, as we have said some six-and-a-half acres in extent and there is a siding from the Midland Railway running right into the works. On the frontage to the Kimpton Road have been erected eleven workmen's dwellings in addition to residences for the two foremen and a caretaker, whilst Vauxhall House, a residence of very pretty design and admirably arranged, is occupied by the Works Manager and is situated at the main entrance to the works. ❜

*A photograph of a painting owned by Messrs John Mowlem & Co. It shows the Thames river tug* John Mowlem *powered by a marine engine built by Alexander Wilson's company at Vauxhall Iron Works, Lambeth, about 1870. Marine engines were produced by the company from 1857 until 1907 when motor cars became its sole output.*

*This large power unit for a twin-paddle steamer was a typical product of Alexander Wilson. The plate on the unit says Alexander Wilson & Co, Vauxhall Iron Works, 1877.*

*The district of Vauxhall, London, at the turn of the century. The London factory moved to Luton in 1905 due to problems over the lease and lack of space. Complete cars had to be brought out of the factory basement by hoist – and the telegraphic address was Wellhole, London!*

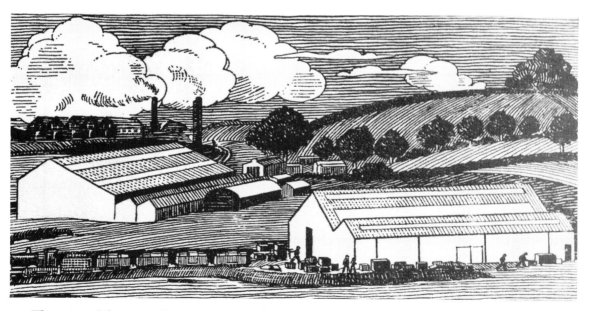

*The original factory at Luton in 1905, which occupied a six-and-a-half acre site and employed between 160 and 200 hands according to pressure of work. The buildings on the extreme left are those of the West Hydraulic Engineering Co.*

*Vauxhall employees (above) pose for an official photograph outside their new Luton headquarters in Kimpton Road, 1905. Total workforce at this time was about 160. At the end of the First World War, Vauxhall built imposing new offices on a site immediately in front of its factory and facing Kimpton Road. The picture (below) taken in April 1951 shows the time is 5 o'clock and some of the 12,000-plus workforce are leaving for home by bus or bicycle. Today the staff that worked in the old offices in Kimpton Road have moved into Griffin House, the new head office, in Osborne Road. One feature of the old offices was a fine wood-panelled hall where a 1905 Vauxhall was always on display. Today the old offices are occupied by the Chamber of Commerce.*

# Manufacturing

Albert Mann joined Vauxhall in 1922 at the age of 20 having pedalled ten miles from Silsoe to the Kimpton Road factory for the job interview. The following article about him appeared in the *Luton News* Vauxhall Souvenir Supplement, March 29 1995:

❛ "It was a very small place then, compared to what it was later," recalled Albert, who is now a cheery 93-year-old great-grandfather, living in the Ferndale Residential Home at Flitwick. "I was put on to woodwork straightaway. Mostly, I did doors and door-making. We worked in pairs. We were doing touring cars, with side screens.

"I think I started on the Kington. It was a nice job, a big five-seater, the biggest they made in those days. There was also the Merton, a two-seater, and I worked on one Prince Henry. "They were all built by hand, from aluminium and wood. All the woodwork was cut out already and you had to trim it up and put it together. Making a door from scratch, hanging it and getting it ready for panelling, was an eight-hour job. You only did one a day, but they were good doors! There were about 50 working in our shop. The bodies were on trestles on a track. We used to have a bench along the side and trestles up the middle and they used to move the bodies around until the woodwork was done. Then the other gang would start on the aluminium. If we did 18 in a week, we'd had a good week."

Among the prestigious cars produced by Vauxhall when Albert joined were the 23/60, with a four-cylinder over-head valve engine, which cost £895 in 1922, and in the same year, the cheaper 14/40, also with a four-cylinder engine, priced at £650.

Albert remembers working on the famous 30/98, which was introduced in 1913, re-launched in 1919, when it cost £2,000, and

re-introduced once more in 1923.

The atmosphere in the body shop was formal and supervision was strict. As always, however, there were jokers who couldn't resist the odd prank.

On pay day wages were handed out in round tins, each with a hinged lid, with the employee's name stamped into the metal. Chuckled Albert: "They used to bring the tins into the office on a wooden tray. You lined up for them, and there was a wooden box with a hole in it. You put your tin back in there when you'd emptied it.

"But some of these fellows would have the tin out of your hand before you knew you'd lost it. They would put it in a vice, with the money inside, and nearly flatten it! You had to cut it to get it open. They had so many squashed, they decided to throw them all away and bring in pay packets instead."

Luckily, the hard-earned pay emerged from the mangled metal intact. Albert's pay then, he recalled, was one shilling and nine-pence an hour, just under 9p in decimal money. His hours were from 8 am to 5.30 pm, usually six days a week, and there was plenty of overtime.

Buses were unreliable, so he cycled to work each day from Silsoe. He explained: "The buses were the old open-top double deckers, with solid wheels. They did 12 mph." Albert did eventually begin travelling to work by bus, for three shillings and four pence a week (just under 17p), a large chunk of the five shillings (25p) he kept for spending money.

Later, he got on his bike again and joined a group of fellow Vauxhall cyclists who enjoyed the fun and banter of their commuting journeys.

Albert moved from Silsoe to Maulden and finally to Flitwick, where he and his late wife Elsie, who he married in 1925, lived in Kings Road for 32 years.

In the early days, Elsie would sometimes prepare a midday meal in an aluminium basin with a twist-lock lid. Albert cycled in with the basin in a case behind him, ready for the obliging canteen staff to reheat at lunchtime.

Changes blew in from across the Atlantic when General Motors took over the company in 1925, and Vauxhall began concentrating on lower-priced cars, starting with the six-cylinder Cadet, which cost £298 in 1930. The 1931 model was the first British car with a synchromesh gearbox, and that year, the first Bedford truck was also produced.

Albert left for a time, in 1929, to start his own garage in Luton's Cromwell Road, but returned to Vauxhall in 1933 and stayed with the firm until his retirement, in 1967.

"General Motors started making all-steel jobs," he recalled. "When I went back, I was a jig and tool maker. I got on better with iron and steel than I did with wood. I was really interested in jig making, and in the different types of steel you used for different jobs. I loved that job at the finish.

"I used to make jigs for everything that came along. There were improvements all the time. The mass production was entirely different to what we were doing in the old Vauxhall days, and we started making as many as 400 a day."

Albert's sons, Colin, 61, and David, 59, joined the firm as apprentices and became production engineers, between them working for Vauxhall for a total of 77 years. Looking back, Albert is proud to have seen Vauxhall's growth into a manufacturing giant, constantly upgrading technology.

He said: "If I had my way, I'd do it all over again." **,**

The basic problem for Vauxhall before 1930 was that of low productivity, which prevented effective price competition with producers such as Austin, Morris and Ford.

By 1925 Vauxhall had made an attempt to organize the works along a quasi-assembly line for the insertion of the engine and other adjacent parts of the chassis. In reality production was slow compared with other companies' and was more like a more efficient version of the old batch system of production. Much bench and batch production work was carried out.

The capacity of the works was about 30 chassis a week. In October 1925 the *Automobile Engineer* commented: "The company have managed to introduce some of the best features of mass production into an organization which preserves individuality and is sufficiently flexible to cater for the customer who is prepared to pay rather more than the price of a mass produced car." There were no automatic conveyors and much of the work was man-handled into assembly position.

It was not until 1929, after GM had agreed to the expansion of Vauxhall, that the beginnings of a modern mass assembly line were introduced. Conveyors were used in chassis and engine assembly, although moving assembly lines were not introduced until 1933. In 1930 the plant was capable of producing 75 chassis per day.

The 1929 re-organization still meant that components of each type of vehicle had to be manufactured in batches. This meant commercial vehicles were produced for some days, or even weeks, before tooling was changed for the production of cars. During the erection both cars and commercial vehicles were assembled on the chassis line simultaneously, although separate frame assembly lines and body building shops were provided.

In February 1933 £500,000 was spent in re-organizing the works. Two parallel assembly lines were installed, one for passenger cars and one for commercial vehicles. Both lines incorporated machine operated continuous conveyors for engine, chassis and final assembly.

The re-organization resulted in the output of 150 chassis a day which was double the 1930 figure. Managing Director Charles Bartlett saw the re-organization as the last stage in the transformation of Vauxhall into a mass producer. He stated that the replanned works were the final break with the company's past association with "old selective and expensive cars".

Between 1933 and 1937 Vauxhall continually re-organized and extended its plant. During that time floor space doubled from 20 to 41 acres. In 1935 K Block was built covering six-and-a-half acres. This block was mainly concerned with machining and assembly of axles, body finishing and general assembly.

'In 1935 *A Souvenir of Vauxhall* was published and given as a memento of a visit to the factory in Luton. This is an extract from that publication:

‘On the purely scientific side our metallurgists and scientists in our own laboratories determine the exact specifications of the materials we need for our multitudinous purposes and later test every consignment to assure themselves that the supplies attain to their standards. Also they are continuously engaged upon research work which results in the improvements in the trucks and cars we manufacture.

But the other studies are equally important in that the methods and times and costs of production are scientifically considered so that selling prices can be fixed accurately and competitively. It would be unwise and unfair to permit manufacturing operations and their costs merely to happen.

Every activity is organised scientifically and then studied and timed to ensure expedition with the minimum of manual effort. Only by the regular application of such methods can high quality cars and trucks be produced and sold at low prices.

Research and study of all phases intertwine in the Vauxhall organisation in a way that would astonish those who laid the foundation of Vauxhall reputation.

We need only give a few figures to indicate the responsibilities of those who sit regularly on the committees. Over £4,750,000 are spent yearly on materials, and this money goes into scores of towns throughout the country. Over £1,500,000 are paid out in wages to more than 7,000 employees.

More than ten per cent of the population

of Luton depend upon Vauxhall Motors Limited – and behind them are tradesmen and others who benefit.

The Production Control Division alone is involved in over 1,000,000 calculations each month after the Forecast Committee has decided what shall be made. All these and other matters are considered and decided by committees and it is remarkable how accurate are their decisions.

As further illustrations of the work involved, there are more than 7,500 complete parts in a Vauxhall car, involving 15,000 separate operations and about 11,000 different inspection checks.

All that we have stated is but a scanty sketch of the wealth of consideration that surrounds the actual operations you saw when you walked round. Yet, these brief references will suggest something of the community mind that contributes to the smooth activity which characterizes the work done in the shops. Much of this you no doubt sensed but did not see.

And now we will recall your tour. You started at a Goods Inwards section through which, including five others, an average of nearly 300 tons of material entered the factory each working day last year.

Then you went into that important Gear Shop where Synchro-Mesh and other gears are cut before they are submitted to the highly technical processes of heat treatment. Do you remember the "Silence Room" for ensuring the quietness of the gears, and were you able to catch the explanation of how heat treatment controls the degree of hardness and softness of parts according to the various duties they have to perform – how the outsides of gear wheels, for instance, are hardened to prevent wear while their insides remain soft to withstand shock?

Then you passed through what we call the Bar Shop, and saw lengthy machines being fed with bars of various sizes. From these machines drop bolts and bushes and other small items with an almost amusing regularity, after being shaped and fashioned by tools that come into play by automatic means, making holes or adding threads according to the will of those who set them up.

You then visited the Engine Shop where the Vauxhall and Bedford engines are built. You probably noticed those multiple drilling machines which drill over 60 holes at once. They are an example of the economies that allow Vauxhall Cars and Bedford Trucks to be sold at such attractive prices.

You also saw the Engine Test benches where the engines are tested under applied power and then under their own power and re-tested in various ways. There is too much to mention about this important shop, full of activity, and one in which you, no doubt, could have spent more time. But you passed into the Axle Shop where axle and frame fittings were being assembled or prepared for the final assembly line.

Then there was the shop where "Riding is turned into Gliding" – the independent front wheel assembly section; an interesting feature of the tour and responsible for the most welcome contribution to comfortable travel yet made.

Then the Saw Mill was visited, and you glanced at some of the remarkable mechanized woodwork machines and the operators who were handling ingenious contrivances, called jigs, which enable them to fashion wood to the necessary shapes and to turn out astonishing quantities with a slickness that cannot be understood unless seen. From there you went down the road to the mammoth Press Shop with its tremendous presses and all the din associated with the finishing of metal work.

We illustrate one of those large presses which fashion wings and other items with tremendous pressure. Associated with this work are those ingenious machines used to "wire" the edges of wings and various smaller presses and spot welders and the band saws and so on and on.

Perhaps that Press Shop made a greater impression than some of the other operations because the work done is so easy to understand although it is astonishing to realize that wings which, in some works, take days to make by hand, are here formed in seconds.

You also saw the bodies for Vauxhall cars being built with the aid of those large jigs which might be described as skeleton moulds, in which the body frames are accurately made to fit so that the body panels may be applied without distortion, thus squeaks and rattles are unlikely when you take the car on to the road.

You probably paused a moment or two to glance at chemical washing, enamelling and the baking which follows at a temperature of 500 degrees Fahrenheit.

The next operation was that of making commercial bodies and what we call paint and trim operations. Some of these activities will be remembered by you because they are so familiar in the home. Everybody has seen painting done, and sewing and the other trim operations; but have you seen them carried out in such facile and comprehensive manner before?

Then, as one of the last visits of your tour, you went to the final assembly lines, first of all visiting the noisy chassis-riveting lines where red hot rivets are pneumatically hammered into position, and electrical welding operations carried out prior to the transfer of the frame to the long conveyors, where all the units and assemblies are fitted with deliberation by numerous men who work on both sides of the lines.

These conveyors move slowly forward while the parts are fitted, and you watched the bare chassis gradually built up until, on its own wheels, it arrived at the Brake Setting machine, where the brakes are so accurately adjusted that each Vauxhall Car or Bedford Truck can take the road for test. We feel there is no need for a detailed reminder of that quite remarkable sight.

Perhaps you followed one of the cars from a final conveyor line to the Factory Final Inspection Department where men work who have been educated to diagnose sounds and symptoms. They follow very carefully determined lines of diagnosis and make a final inspection of all those parts of the car or truck that already have been inspected again and again during the individual processing and then in the assembly activities.

In this somewhat less interesting shop, because only completed cars seem to exist, there was that very amusing machine used to produce the shocks of the road, giving irregular and independent vibrations to each road wheel, and reproducing abnormally bad road conditions. It is this machine that tells trained men, among other things, whether the body jigs have done their work and the body is free from squeaks and rattles. It also is a guide for future designing.

The cars are then driven by skilled drivers who report symptoms to yet more expert inspectors, who again go over the cars and trucks and prepare them for car storage, and for our 700 dealers and thousands of buyers. They rest only a few hours, because much room is needed to store motor vehicles, and it means hopeless congestion if they are not moved as quickly as they are stored. **)**

By 1938 the Luton Plant covered over 53 acres. The most significant development was that in welding technique. The entire body shell could now be built without bolts or rivets by a series of flash welding operations. This was organized on a continuous basis with a time cycle of six minutes per shell and most of the operations were mechanized to eliminate human error. Output and productivity were considerably increased and the welding of a 25 hp model was reduced from 35 minutes to two minutes.

The Vauxhall site was unsuitable for a large modern factory. This was because it was situated on lower slopes of the Chiltern Hills. This made expansion difficult as large volumes of earth had to be removed from the slopes to erect new buildings. It was therefore decided in 1938 to purchase land in Dunstable and erect a plant for the production of commercial vehicles.

In 1948 Vauxhall began a £14 million reorganization on streamlining production. Two car models, namely the Velox and Wyvern, were now produced. Vauxhall was committed to a programme of one wheel base, one shell and a choice of two engines.

During the last few years the company has spent more than £100 million on modernizing the Luton plant. In 1994 a £22 million upgrade took place. The Luton factory's body trim and final assembly units, covering an area of 600,000 sq ft, were completely transformed. During the company's annual three-week summer holiday, 2,000 tons of steelwork were stripped out. Two of the plant's car assembly lines, which produced Cavaliers, were replaced with a state-of-the-art conveyor system and new robots.

Some 4,000 people are employed in the assembly plant at Luton compared with 28,000 in the 1960s. By early 1995 the production line was able to produce 44 cars per hour or nearly 800 cars per day or about 130,000 per year. By the end of this year (1996) it is hoped production will have risen to 72 cars per hour with an annual output of 215,000 vehicles. Ten per cent of the production line staff are women. Material is imported from all over the world, mainly from Europe but also from as far away as Australia and Japan. Many local firms supply components, for example shock absorbers are supplied by a Dunstable firm. Material arrives by truck. The stock is in use within six hours of being delivered. Unloading time is one hour and it is then held in temporary storage for another five hours. A lean material system is used whereby material is kept in storage for as little time as possible. This Japanese style of working has extended to team work in which every team member is capable of doing each other's job and jobs are rotated within the teams.

In the autumn of 1995 the new Vectra replaced the Cavalier, going on sale in Britain at around 500 dealerships on October 18 1995. About 400 German-built robots are used to make the car at the Luton plant, which is the lead plant out of three factories that are making it. Vauxhall, which is the major employer in Luton, spent £136 million modernizing its Luton factory in readiness for the Vectra. The Vectra hatchback is assembled for the UK market and the Opel Vectra hatchback for overseas markets.

*Motor work bay at Vauxhall Iron Works. Two bays were devoted to motor work with another two used for marine engineering. In the motor bay the chassis were laid out on wooden trestles and slowly the cars were built up in-situ. The assemblers would have had the many parts brought to them. In the background are runs of overhead line shafting, with driving belts to each machine. One of the biggest problems in the Machine Shop was the danger of accidents to the workers, as virtually no belt guards were fitted.*

*By 1920 the motor shop had a simple track on which the chassis were assembled. Parts were brought to the production line in bulk, and stored there, rather than using the modern method of bringing in parts only for each particular car.*

*Aerial view of the Vauxhall factory, early 1930s. At this time the factory covered more than 31 acres of floor area and employed well over 7,000 people.*

*Machining items for gearbox assembly in the gear shop. This view of the middle bay illustrates the Vauxhall maxim "orderliness means thoroughness", 1930s.*

*A corner of the press shop in the 1930s showing the 450 ton giant presses which pressed flat metal sheets into wings, panels and bonnets. These huge machines were controlled by a simple lever, which responded to at most a finger touch. It was changing the dies used in these machines which made them so expensive to re-tool for a new model.*

*Part of the sheet metal finishing department, 1930s.*

*Laboratory, late 1920s. Here all metals were tested to ensure they complied with the specifications laid down by the design engineers.*

*The drawing office, 1930. This is where new models and improvements to existing types were drawn up in plan form so they could be interpreted by staff in the manufacturing process. The drawing office was the nerve centre of operations.*

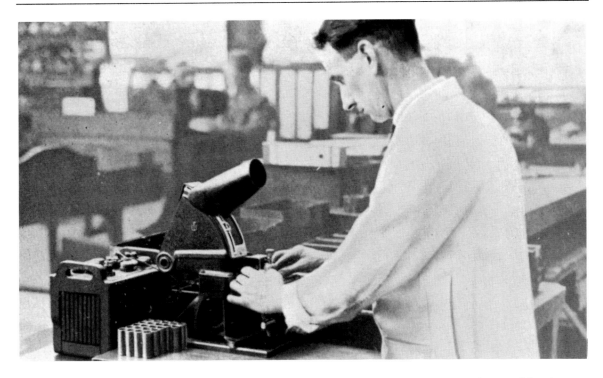

*An inspector uses an optimeter to grade piston or gudgeon pins to one ten thousandth of an inch, 1930s.*

*The middle section of the saloon body assembly line with "feeders" on each side. The moving assembly line had arrived. By 1930 true mass production methods were being applied by all the major British manufacturers, and Vauxhall of course was no exception.*

*The finish of the assembly line with a Light Six on the brake adjustment machine. It was then test-driven by an expert inspector.*

*Racing motorist Kay Petrie takes a look together with officials at the new L-type 6-cylinder Velox, August 1948. Some of the workers who helped manufacture it stand in the background.*

In 1929 the entire UK General Motors manufacturing operation was transferred to Luton from Hendon. Hendon became a centre for sales distribution and service operations. Pictured above is the Part Stores counter at Hendon. The Vauxhall Express Parts Service vans are pictured below. Both pictures were taken in the early 1930s. A few years later both departments were transferred to Luton.

*In 1955-7 Vauxhall Motors spent £36 million to double car production. About one-and-a-half million tons of chalk and clay were excavated leaving a white plain as large as 12 football pitches, ready for the erection of a 1,600,000 sq ft building. The spoil extended Luton Airport by 12 acres, reclaimed 32 acres of marsh in Luton Hoo Park and contoured for easier ploughing 32 acres of undulating pasture in Lea Valley.*

*Block AA, early 1950s. At the time of its construction in 1948, this was one of the largest buildings in England. It was filled with modern machine tools and assembly conveyors, and produced engines, gearboxes and rear-axles for Vauxhall and Bedford cars, trucks and vans. It is said that the steelwork (1285 ft long and 480 ft wide) was imported from America where it either had been previously erected as, or was intended to be, part of a General Motors' aircraft plant during the Second World War, manufacturing the Boeing B29, the famous Flying Fortress bomber. The 5,000 tons of steelwork were loaded on a ship bound for London docks. Unfortunately a dockers' strike was in progress in London so that the steel remained on board and returned to the US East coast. It later came back to London for unloading and transportation to Luton by road.*

*In 1985 there was an announcement that the next new car at Luton would largely be built by robot power. The production line at Ellesmere Port had already been successfully automated without job losses or union objections. However, people are still required as can be seen by these two pictures. The car involved is the Cavalier and a transponder which identifies the model to the robot can be seen attached to the Cavalier, above. This small metal cannister emits a signal so that, for example, the car is painted with the correct colour. The computerized system and robots mean that it is commonplace to see a red five-door hatchback being followed by a blue four-door diesel. Each vehicle is a Cavalier, but each vehicle is individually put together to ensure the customer gets the exact version he or she has ordered.*

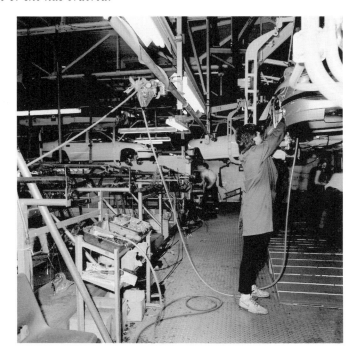

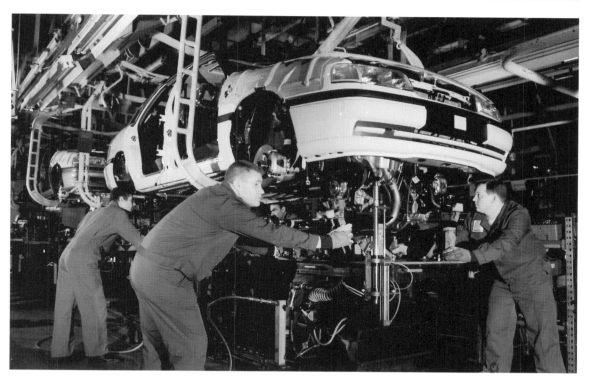

*A Cavalier body unites with mechanical components. The Cavalier, manufactured at Luton since 1977, attained its highest market share of 10.5 per cent in 1984. Hundreds of Luton staff have worked on the three Cavalier marks. It ceased production in 1995 when the 1,678,368th model burst through a poster with a reproduction of the painting,* The Laughing Cavalier, *looking on.*

*Door trim area.*

# Some of the Cars

The first Vauxhall car appeared in 1903, price 130 guineas (£136.50). The two-seater had a 989 cc engine, tiller steering, single chain drive and a two-speed epicyclic gearbox with no reverse. Top speed was 25 mph and 43 cars were produced. A four-seater model was also available. The two extra passengers sat over the engine, ahead of the driver. In February 1904 a more powerful 6 hp 1039 version, which could seat four, was brought out with a reverse gear. Its price was £150. In September 1904 a steering wheel replaced the tiller. In November a three-cylinder model, the 12/14, costing £375 was produced.

The 18 hp four-cylinder Vauxhall appeared in 1905 price £475. This was the first Vauxhall with flutes down each side of the bonnet starting from the radiator, a trademark for the next 54 years. In 1906 Vauxhall's new motor engineer, Laurence Pomeroy, was mainly responsible for the introduction of a 12/16 hp four-cylinder car, selling for £375.

In 1908 the RAC 2,000 miles trial provided Pomeroy with the opportunity of designing a new model incorporating amongst other things "an accelerator pedal instead of a lever on the steering wheel, operating wedges to accelerate the engine by giving more lift to the inlet valves".

During 1909 two new models were introduced: the A-type four-speed 20 hp four-cylinder factory version of the RAC 2,000 miles winner and a smaller B-type version, the 16 hp with three speeds.

In 1910 the "30" appeared. This was a luxury car with six cylinders. The following year the new sporting car, a 55 bhp C-type 20 hp Prince Henry was on sale at £485. A new 25 hp D-type was introduced during 1912. In 1913 the famous 30/98 was introduced. This E-type was a 25 hp design.

The D-type became the British Army's standard staff car during the 1914-18 war.

By 1920 the E-type had a 29.47 hp figure and Vauxhall sold the car with a guaranteed 100 mph top speed. It was a development of the C-type Prince Henry.

In 1922 the 14 hp M-type, later known as 14/40, was introduced. Priced around £650 it was aimed at the non-sporting ordinary driver. In 1925 came the much more expensive 25/70 S-type, a six-cylinder car with a price tag of £1,350–£1,675. The car was not a great success. The 20/60 followed in 1927. This replaced the 14/40. The 20/60 had a six-cylinder engine with a rating of 21 hp.

In 1930 the T-type, also known as the Silent 80 because it had a direct-drive, silent third gear, was launched. This 23 hp cost up to £750. However, by the end of year Vauxhall had brought out the £280 Cadet. The Cadet was designed specifically for the fast-growing market in low-priced family cars. Two versions were offered, 17 hp and 26 hp six-cylinder engines.

Its successor, the Light Six model, was introduced in 1933 in 12 and 14 hp versions starting at an incredibly low price of £195. It was a big success and in its first year accounted for 40 per cent of all 14 hp new car registrations in Britain. The following year saw the Big Six, 20 hp price £325 and 27 hp price £550. For 1937 the Big Sixes were replaced by the GY 25 priced at £298 and capable of over 80 mph.

In 1937 a million pounds was invested in order to produce the famous 10 hp H models. The car was an immediate success. It broke new ground in that it was Vauxhall's first mass produced car. It had a *monocoque* or integral chassis and body construction. Being a light car it was capable of returning well over 40 miles to the gallon.

It cost £168. The 12 hp I-type was introduced in 1938 along with the 14 hp J-model.

During the 1939-45 war, 5,640 Churchill tanks were produced by Vauxhall in Luton. When car production resumed after the war Vauxhall continued with H, I and J models. It was not until 1948 that the L-type Wyvern/Velox models were launched. The following is a list of models and achievements which followed after 1948:

1951 E-type Wyvern/Velox introduced, in 1.5 and 2.25 litre forms.

1953 Jubilee of the Vauxhall car. Company builds its millionth vehicle.

1954 £36 million plant expansion project announced. E-type Cresta launched.

1957 First Victor models, 1.5 litre F-type saloons. PA 6-cylinder models replace the E-types.

1958 Victor estate car offered – first factory-built Vauxhall estate car.

1959 Vauxhall Motors produces its two-millionth vehicle. Further expansion announced – new car plant at Ellesmere Port.

1961 FB Victors introduced.

1962 PB 6-cylinder models launched.

1963 HA Viva 1-litre saloons launched.

1964 New Victor 101 (FC series) models. 3.3 litre engine for PB Velox-Cresta.

1965 PC 6-cylinder models introduced. 250,000th Viva produced.

1966 HB Viva models; built at Ellesmere Port.

1967 FD Victor range – new ohc engines.

1968 Ventora variant introduced; three new FD Victor estate cars. HB Viva 4-door saloons. Work started on new Millbrook proving ground.

1970 HC Vivas launched.

1971 Millionth Viva produced. Firenza coupe announced. Dealer Team Vauxhall formed.

1972 FE 1800 and 2300 Victors introduced.

1973 Magnum 1800 and 2300 models announced.

1975 Chevette hatchbacks launched. Cavalier saloons and coupe introduced.

1976 VX saloons/estates replace FE models. Five saloons, one estate car, added to Chevette range.

1977 Cavalier production begins at Luton. Cavalier 1300 model introduced.

1978 75th anniversary of Vauxhall cars. New models–Carlton, Royale, Cavalier Sports Hatch. Equus "concept" sports car shown publicly.

1979 New Vauxhall Astra front-wheel-drive models announced for 1980 season.

1981 New Vauxhall J Cavalier launched. First Vauxhall Astras built at Ellesmere Port.

1982 Diesel option for Vauxhall Astra and Cavalier; Cavalier 2-door convertible announced.

1983 Vauxhall Nova launched, plus Astra GTE.

1984 £100 million investment announced by GM in Vauxhall car-build facilities. All-new Astra range launched.

1985 £90 million paint shop being built at Luton. 4 x 4 Astra rally car. Belmont models announced; half-millionth Vauxhall Cavalier sold in UK.

1986 Vauxhall announces Astra convertible; new Carlton models.

1987 New paint shop in operation at Luton car plant. Vauxhall Carlton voted Car of the Year. New Senator models; Nova GTE launched.

1988 Vauxhall-Lotus racing car announced, plus 16-valve Astra GTE. Cavalier sales pass million mark. All-new Cavalier range introduced. Vauxhall Motors net profit of £152 million.

1989 Cavalier 4 x 4 available. Astra range grows to 32 models. £50 million modernisation of Luton plant area begins.

1991 Frontera launched, Vauxhall's first "recreational" vehicle (made by IBC Vehicles).

1992 Record output achieved. Despite recession Vauxhall becomes first UK manufacturer to equip all petrol engine cars with catalytic converters.

1993 Corsa comes in as replacement for the Nova and sporty Calibra appears.

1994 Launch of Omega, executive-type car, and Tigra coupe.

1995 The Vectra, replacement for Cavalier announced.

---

Note: Dates given for new-model introductions are, wherever possible, the dates when the models were publicly announced. For many years these dates were chosen to coincide with the London Motor Show, usually October or November. In many cases the new models were not available in the showrooms until the beginning of the following year.

*The first Vauxhall car, produced in 1903. The car was steered by a tiller. Its two forward speeds were worked from a device on the steering column. No reverse gear was necessary as the law did not require cars under 5 cwt to be fitted with one. One privately owned two-seater model has survived and is on loan to the Science Museum in London. Its registration number is A 719.*

*The first Vauxhalls were small two-seaters. They had neither windscreen nor roof. Top speed was 25 mph and they cost 130 guineas (£136.50). This 5 hp car had no reverse gear!*

*This 6 hp, single-cylinder vehicle was one of about 70 built in 1904 by the Vauxhall Iron Works in London, the forerunner of Vauxhall Motors. It has competed regularly, since 1950, in the London to Brighton run. The only time the car failed to complete the rally was in 1964 when the back axle broke just outside Brighton.*

*The Prince Henry appeared in 1911. This C-type took part in the famous Prussian Reliability Trial and was named after the Prussian Royal of that name. It was elegant, expensive and fast and credited by many as the first British sports car. The original 19.9 hp engine was later replaced (for the 1913 models) by a 22.5 hp unit. Chassis price alone excluding body was £485.*

*A 25 hp staff car now in the Vauxhall collection. This particular 1918-built model may never have seen active service abroad. However, nearly 2,000 25 hp D-type Vauxhalls were built for the Services between 1914 and 1918.*

*A 1925 Carlton limousine, costing £1,295, one of several OD models. A standard feature of this car was front-wheel brakes. It was not until 1978 that the name Carlton appeared again in the Vauxhall range. It is interesting to note that in the 1920s Vauxhall ran an instruction class at Luton. For three guineas, a week's course for chauffeurs and owner-drivers was run on "the management and driving of Vauxhall cars".*

*The elegant dashboard of the 1926 Vauxhall 30/98. Cars of this type with their polished wood, gleaming brass and leather seats were coveted by car-lovers everywhere.*

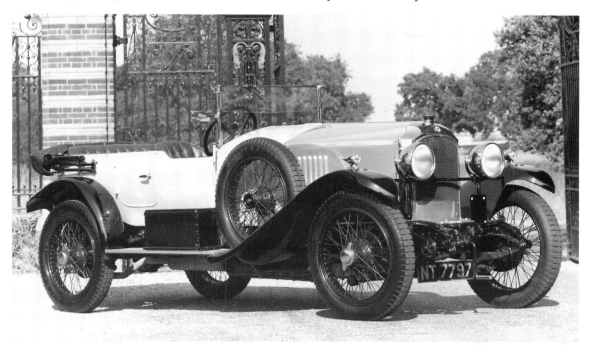

*Laurence H. Pomeroy designed this fast touring sports car. Pictured is a 1926 OE-type 30/98. No one knows why it was called the 30/98. The car raced at 23.8 hp. Between 1920 and 1923 the E and OE type models scored over 70 "firsts" and 52 "seconds" in major hill-climbs and speed trials. In 1932 a 1926 OE model won the Brooklands Gold Star, averaging 109.46 mph. The cars were road tested on a race track at Brooklands and each carried a "guaranteed" 100 mph performance.*

In 1930 the Cadet was launched as a result of the 1925 Vauxhall General Motors' merger. It was designed specifically for the low-priced family car market. The Cadet came in two 6-cylinder engine versions, 17 hp and 26 hp. The cheapest model was the standard 17 hp saloon which cost £280. There were only three forward speeds.

A 1933 Light Six shows its stamina by getting into difficult places. On dealer launch day June 14 1933, 250 Light Sixes were available for Vauxhall dealers to drive away from Luton. This was an unprecedented achievement in the British motor industry. Available in 12 hp and 14 hp versions the 6-cylinder car cost £195 and £215 respectively. The 14 hp was the more popular with the Light Six accounting for 40 per cent of all 14 hp new-car registrations in 1933.

*The ten-thousandth Vauxhall "10" leaves the factory just five months after the introduction of the model, 1937.*

*In 1954 the name Cresta appeared on an extra-luxury version of the 2.25 litre Velox. This car is a 1956 Cresta.*

In October 1948 the first new post-war models arrived, the L-type Velox and Wyvern. These models had steering column gear change and the Velox (above) had a brand new 2.25 litre 6-cylinder engine with a top speed of 75 mph. The Wyvern had a 4-cylinder 1.5 litre engine. Both models shared a common body shell. The name of Wyvern model (below) was a surprising choice. Many people have since referred to the Vauxhall emblem as the Wyvern, whereas it is the heraldic griffin. The L-type had a rear-hinged bonnet; until that time vehicles had had their bonnets split, and hinged in the middle. Pressmen were soon to point out that "the makers have made no provision for a starting handle", as the radiator of the Velox got in the way. These L-type models were the first ever to have steering column gear change. They remained in production until 1951 when the E-type Wyvern/Velox range was introduced in 1.5 and 2.25 litre forms.

*In late 1957 the E-type Wyvern/Velox/Cresta models were replaced by long, sleek PA Sixes. The Velox and Cresta (pictured) took the 2.25 litre over-square engine. In 1959 the two-millionth Vauxhall rolled off the production line in the form of a PA Cresta. This year also saw the dropping of the traditional flutes from the body sides. They had started life on the bonnet of the 1905 Vauxhall.*

*New 6-cylinder models were on show at the 1962 London Motor Show. The PB Velox and Cresta (pictured) inherited the 2.5 litre engine of earlier PA Sixes.*

*Early 1957 saw the new 1.5 litre F-type Victor model.*

*The FB Victor appeared in 1961 with a 1508 cc 4-cylinder engine. In 1963 engine size increased to 1594 cc. The FB Victor was produced until late 1964, by which time over 328,000 had been sold. Four speeds with floor change became a catalogued option while the de luxe saloons came with heaters and dual-note horns as standard. Even before this model the Victor had become Britain's top export car. With the Victor, Vauxhall made its first export bid in America with Pontiac dealers handling the Victor.*

*The FC Victor 101 models appeared in 1964. One distinctive feature was the curved side windows which gave greater shoulder room.*

*In 1963 Vauxhall broke into the small car market with the 1-litre HA Viva, which was designed at Luton. The works were tooled at a cost of £5 million. This new small car had a top speed of over 80 mph and a petrol consumption of 42 mpg. It cost £527 which included purchase tax of £91. Many of the cars were produced at the new Ellesmere Port plant which brought out its first Viva on June 1 1964. The Viva went on to become Vauxhall's first million-seller. By 1969 the Viva was commanding nearly 11 per cent of all home-market sales.*

*In 1967 the FD Victor model was launched with a new overhead-cam engine, in 1599 and 1975 cc versions. A standard feature was the energy-absorbing steering column with the option of a 4-speed floor-change gearbox.*

*Vauxhall's new boss, Alex Rhea, a 56-year-old Texan, sits in the driving seat of the newest Vauxhall Viva at the press preview of the Earls Court Motor Show, October 1970. This Viva de luxe 4-door was on sale for £675 ex-factory with a total price of £883 10s 10d (£883.54) including purchase tax.*

*Geneva in March 1975 saw the unveiling of the 3-door Chevette hatchback model with a 1256 cc engine. It was a cousin of the German-built Opel Kadett with its floorpan, suspension, screen and doors all being Opel. The Chevette was a derivation of the American giant's T car, which had appeared a year-and-a-half earlier. The basic car design was tailored to suit a country's specific requirement in trim, transmission and power format. The small T car first appeared in Brazil in 1974 as a Chevrolet.*

*In 1981 the J-type Cavalier arrived. The 15 original models offered 1.3 and 1.6 litre ohc engines. On launch day, September 17, nearly 700 Cavaliers were driven away from the Luton plant by UK dealers. The Cavalier was a blinding success and transformed Vauxhall from a company that faced oblivion into a world-beater.*

*The 180 mph Lotus Carlton (Lotus Omega in other markets), 1990. The car was designed by Lotus around the Carlton's straight six. The 377 hp car has a six-speed gearbox and features two turbos with charge cooling. The Carltons and Omegas arrived at the Lotus factory in Norwich where the engine, gearbox, diff and interior trim were replaced. Ten days later the standard car had been transformed into a supercar.*

*In 1991 the new Astra range was launched in the form of five-door (left), estate (back) and GSi 16v 3-door hatchback models. The new range was developed by General Motors' European technical and design team in Germany and built at Ellesmere Port. All the models have a pollen filter which removes virtually all allergy-causing agents, together with catalytic converter.*

*The 4-wheel drive Frontera recreational vehicle produced at IBC Vehicles, Luton, 1991. The vehicle is based on the Isuzu Rodeo and is available in short (2-door) and long (4-door) wheelbase versions. Over 80 per cent of the Frontera production is destined for continental European markets. IBC is the joint venture manufacturing operation set up in September 1987 by General Motors (who owned 60 per cent) and Isuzu (40 per cent) at the former Bedford van plant in Luton. General Motors Holdings (UK) has now become the owner of three-quarters of IBC with the Isuzu stake down to 25 per cent.*

*The Tigra concept car was the star of the London Motor Show in 1993. Visitors were invited to give their views on this potential new model. It is powered by the Corsa GSi's new 1.6 litre ECOTEC engine. Vauxhall later announced that the Corsa-based Tigra was to go into full production in Spain towards the end of 1994.*

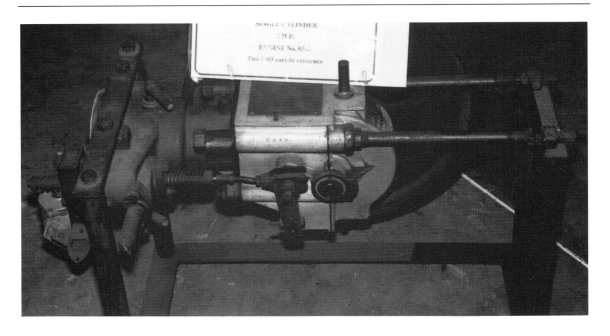

Featured above is a 1903 989 cc horizontal single-cylinder engine with automatic inlet valve which was used on the first Vauxhall production car. The engine produced 5-brake horsepower (bhp) at 900 revolutions per minute (rpm). Top speed was 25 mph. Below is the engine of the Corsa, pictured at the 1993 Motor Show. Models in several engine sizes ranging from 1.2 litre to 1.6 litre 16v are available. The smallest 1195 cc version with four cylinders produces 45 bhp at 4600 rpm and a top speed of 89 mph.

# At War

## 1914-18 War

The start of 1914 saw many sporting successes for the 30/98 and the new 25 hp car in both hill climbs and track events. In Russia, where an agency was opened, a special limousine with gold-plated door handles and radiator was ordered for the Imperial Family.

In August came war and the 25 hp car was thought to be ideal as a military car. Private sales did not stop immediately because War Office negotiations had to be completed. The War Office required a strong, reliable staff car and Vauxhall could turn out seven a week! During 1916 production was raised to eight and this increased to just over eight by the following year. By the end of the war nearly 2,000 of the 25 hp D-type vehicles had been built for the services. They were supplied as open tourers or enclosed limousines, the latter used mainly by senior officers who could not get a Rolls-Royce.

It was not only cars that were being produced by Vauxhall. In 1914, 150 men out of a staff of 700 had joined the colours. With a shortage of male labour thousands of women were recruited to the munitions factories which were located on the outskirts of Luton around Dallow and Chaul End. The Admiralty and War Office awarded large contracts to Vauxhall for the manufacture of fuses. In December 1914 Vauxhall established a special section to make fuses or detonator caps for shells. By 1916 all available land adjoining the works was purchased with a view to building extensions. During the next four years millions of fuses were turned out by women and girls.

## Second World War Efforts

One of the most spectacular achievements of the company was the saga of the now legendary Churchill tank. With Britain threatened by invasion, the Army had fewer than 100 tanks in 1940. The Government asked Vauxhall to design and build a new one – and quickly.

Normally that would have been a four-year task. But starting from scratch Vauxhall had the 38-ton Churchill tank ready to go to war within a year. The engine was designed by Vauxhall engineers who had a prototype running in just 89 days. By the end of the war 5,640 Churchill tanks had rumbled off to the defence of the nation.

Bedford "army lorries" – over a quarter of a million of them – also streamed off the Vauxhall assembly lines. Their distinctive square noses were soon a familiar and comforting sight to allied servicemen throughout the world, for they were deployed in every theatre of the war.

Alongside this, highly secret work was done by Vauxhall on mines, torpedoes, radio-location equipment and bombs. Most secret of all was Vauxhall's contribution to the development of the aircraft jet engine. The company made about 95 per cent of the parts for the first 12 aircraft jet engines built in Britain.

Vauxhall's Styling Department became experts in camouflage. And to enable the armed services to confuse the enemy even more they designed inflatable decoy trucks and string-and-canvas decoy aircraft.

At a more workaday level, Vauxhall produced the side panels for five million jerricans, over four million venturi tubes for rocket projectiles, and 750,000 steel helmets.

At one stage the factory turned out 6-pounder armour-piercing shells at the resounding rate of 5,000 a week. Twice the factory was bombed. The worst raid, at 4.50

pm on Friday, August 30 1940, killed 39 employees and seriously injured 40.

## Tanks and Pig

During the 1939-45 war Luton saw many changes. First came the schoolchildren from London, some of whom remained throughout the war, with their teachers. Next came the soldiers such as the Royal Engineers who trained at Vauxhall and other firms.

During the war Vauxhall started making the Churchill tanks and Eric Norris recalls them rattling through Round Green ". . . leaving the marks of their progress on the road behind them".

Another morale-boosting weapon was the pig farm. With the country worried about food supplies and strict rationing in force, fresh meat was always in short supply. The idea of forming a pig section was suggested to the Vauxhall Recreation Club. A pig farm on St Anne's Hill was established and eventually had about 50 pigs with one pig-keeper. The canteen used to save all the scrapings from plates to put into the pig-swill bins sent to the pig farm. Every so often a number of pigs were killed, with half going to the Ministry of Food for the war effort, the other half for the Vauxhall canteen. When news leaked out that pork and pork dripping were on the menu there would be a rush to the canteen and the latecomers who missed out were always causing rows. In the end the general council of the Rec Club had to have a meeting especially to find ways of sharing the pork and pork dripping as fairly as possible.

## Engineer

In the Second World War Churchill tanks were concentrated in Army tank brigades and Vauxhall appointed an engineer to each of these brigades. Each individual lived and worked with his brigade and went on exercises with it, living and sleeping rough when necessary. The engineer was made a member of the officers' mess. The Army shifted officers about quite a lot and one engineer who had been attached to the same brigade for about a year, proudly told Vauxhall that he had seen so many officers come and go that he was "now the oldest member of the mess".

As time went on Vauxhall civilian engineers were put into battle dress, given the status of captain and sent all over the world to help the Army look after and operate its Bedfords and Churchills. Engineers were sent to Egypt, Africa, Italy, Belgium, France, Holland, Germany and India. Special concertina window-type wallets were provided by Vauxhall to hold all the passes that the engineers had to carry. On one occasion one man went to a divisional HQ, showed his passes and asked for Major Blank. The soldier on the gate studied the passes very closely. At length he said: "Blimey! All these passes and you only want to see a Major!"

## Tank Movement

When Vauxhall began producing the Churchill tank it was faced with hundreds of problems; one of them was how to move the tanks along the assembly line. This is explained in *An Account of our Stewardship*:

'Imagine a whole string of tanks, stretching the length of the shop; at one end of the line was a tank upon which work was only just beginning; each one in front of it was a little nearer completion, until at the "finishing" end of the line was a vehicle just ready to move off. When that was completed and driven off, all the other tanks behind it had to be moved up "one station" making room for a new beginner at the distant end.

The problem was – how to move them up. At first we used a very powerful winch, chained all the tanks together, and pulled them up that way.

Then we had a better idea. We still chained the tanks together, but each time we finished one, we started up its engine, and made that pull all the others to their new stations. Then it was disconnected, and driven off ready for the Army.

Which gives you some idea of the power of the Bedford flat twin-engine tank. A finished Churchill weighs about 38-tons, and there were 14 tanks on the line, so that one in front had to pull 13 others. But they did not all weigh 38-tons because of course those at the back end were a long way from complete. Actually the average weight was about 25-tons, so that when each newly-completed Churchill was started up, and did the first job of work of its life, it pulled 13 x 25 = 325 tons behind it. **?**

## B.F.'s

During the Second World War Vauxhall produced an unofficial publication *For B.F.'s.* This originated because the Vauxhall liaison engineers were worried by the way that Army drivers would keep the choke control pulled right out long after it should have been pushed back. This practice was extremely bad for the engine and one engineer in particular was constantly pressing the power unit designer to fit a return spring to the choke control so that as soon as the driver let go of the knob it would spring back. A note back to the liaison engineer said: "A spring loaded choke is a retrograde step. I refuse to adopt the suggestion. It is your job to teach the Army fellows not to be such B.F.'s."

One of the Vauxhall directors saw the note and immediately said: "What an idea! There must be a lot of other silly things that drivers do. Let's make a list of them and issue a book called *For B.F.'s*". The book was written and illustrated in an amusing way and became famous through-out the world. Special editions were published in America, Australia and Canada and it was even translated into several languages including Urdu. The B.F. referred to in the booklet was of course always "the other fellow" and not the reader.

## Post War

After the Second World War General Motors personnel coming to work in England were issued with the following information in order to prepare them for their stay in England:

**'**Headquarters of General Motors Ltd (which is mainly a non-vehicle activity) are at 23 Buckingham Gate, London, SW1. At this address are the group Administration and Finance Departments, also Export Operations and U.S. Products Operations – both activities of the Overseas Department. The latter Department also has a warehouse for the U.S. Products Operations at Holmsley, about 100 miles south-west of London.

Readily accessible in and around London are the various General Motors Divisions:

**Frigidaire** are at Hendon, ten miles north of Central London on the Edgware Road.
**Delco-Remy-Hyatt** (automobile electrical equipment and electric motors) are located at Grosvenor Road on the Chelsea Embankment, between Chelsea Bridge and Vauxhall Bridge.
**AC-Sphinx** (spark plugs, oil filters, speedometers, etc) have their factory No 1 at Dunstable on the main A5 road (famous Roman Watling Street) 30 miles out of London and five miles from Luton. Their factory No 2 is at Southampton, 80 miles south-west of London. It is sited in the dock area of Southampton port.

The sole vehicle manufacturing plant in Gt Britain is **Vauxhall Motors** at Luton, some 30 miles north of London, in the county of Bedfordshire. There is a frequent train service to Luton from St Pancras Station, London, whilst the regular road route runs through Hendon, St Albans and Harpenden.

## Living Standards

**Housing:** The shortage of living accommodation is acute, particularly in the London area. It is almost impossible to rent a house unfurnished. Furnished apartments and houses are very scarce in London and the suburbs and all large towns. Apartments, if you can get them, can be rented for either short or long periods, while there are always numbers of unfurnished suburban houses for sale with "vacant possession." Board-residence in houses (as distinct from hotels) is much easier to arrange. Approximate prices are quoted.

**Living Conditions:** Types of houses most popular in Britain are detached and semi-detached and bungalows. The house usually has one upper storey; the bungalow is on one level. Both usually contain six to eight rooms: dining room, bathroom and toilet, and two to four bedrooms. Generally, except in the most modern houses, rooms are not very well fitted with built-in cupboards for clothes storage, etc, and kitchens are rarely equipped to the average American standard. A built-in or detached garage is frequently available but this would not generally be large enough to house an American car.

It is the exception, rather than the rule, for the average home to be on the telephone; demand for telephones is still far from being met. The waiting period is usually over one year.

Plumbing is generally good in houses built since the first world war although in most the bathroom will not include a shower. Insulation against extreme cold has not been taken very seriously, however, and pipe freeze-ups are not uncomnmon in winter. Central heating is not nearly so widely available as in the United States, although many modern houses do have it. Air conditioning is non-existent. Gas, electric, or solid fuel boilers or electric immersion heaters provide hot water supplies. The open coal or log fire is rarely dispensed with during winter months even in centrally heated houses. For quick convenience electric fires are used and modern houses have heating points in all rooms. Electricity is heavily used in the present industrial expansion and fuel cuts are frequent at peak periods during the winter.

Cooking is mostly by gas or electricity, gas being the more popular. Pressure cookers are a post-war innovation and there are good supplies and makes available. Washing machines are being more widely used in face of mounting laundry charges, and good makes are available. Refrigerators which, incidentally, are not yet considered an indispensable part of the British home are fairly easy to obtain. Vacuum cleaners are in good supply.

The general recommendation is, however, that any appliance used to make work easier in the kitchen, should be brought over.

**Domestic Help:** The majority of British housewives do their own household chores, sometimes with the assistance of a daily help for the heavier work two or three mornings a week.

Local Employment Exchanges, as well as Domestic Help Bureaux in most towns, will do all they can to help prospective employers to obtain suitable domestic help.

**Furnishing:** The extent to which Americans will wish to bring their own "bits and pieces" over, will largely depend on the length of their stay in Britain. Generally, it has been found desirable for visitors to leave their larger items until a place has been prepared.

Although the supply of household goods has improved in the last two or three years, good quality sheets, pillow cases, blankets, towelling, etc. might appear to be expensive by American standards. Best value for money is obtained in the "utility" range, in which goods are price-controlled and free of purchase tax. (The mark CC signifies a utility article). Curtaining and other furnishing textiles are in good supply, although utility fabrics patterned on both sides, particularly cottons and chintzes, are scarce.

Latest utility furniture standards are quite high and varieties and qualities are continually improving. There is too, a fair amount of good quality non-utility furniture on the market. Almost without exception, however, styles are different from American interior furnishing.

Floor coverings – linoleum, rubber flooring, carpets and rugs – present little difficulty.

China dinner and tea services are scarce and expensive, most of the Potteries' first class output being exported. Cutlery for the home market does not yet approach pre-war standards or variety. Best quality stainless steel or silver plate is difficult to obtain. Cheap quality electro-plate is more plentiful. Household and cooking utensils, glass ovenware, etc – all can readily be obtained.

**Food**: With the exception of meat (most of which has to be imported) food supplies at present are adequate but only just! Americans will miss, however, the variety of their own diet and the essential "sweetness" of their meals; it is also likely that British cooking will be compared with some Continental and American standards and found less interesting.

Food cartons up to a specified weight limit can be imported by parcel post without duty or tax. It is recommended that canned meat, chicken and fish be included in the despatches from home. Other suggested enclosures are white flour, prepared cake flours, chocolate baking and pudding mixes; and if particular preferences are held towards canned fruits and vegetables, such items as corn, asparagus, beans, fruit salad, apple sauce, plums.

Butchers' meat, bacon, sugar, tea, butter, margarine, cooking fats, certain cheeses, are rationed in Britain. The sugar ration is almost always granulated; cube sugar, when available, must be taken as part of the ration, as must also icing or castor sugar. Flour, milk and bread are plentiful, although milk is sometimes short in the winter and temporary rationing becomes necessary. Pre-war amounts and quality of confectionery have not yet been approached – bakers' ingredients are still restricted. Cakes can be obtained without trouble, but cream and chocolate biscuits (cookies) are not easy to come by.

Unrationed coffee is in good supply. Poultry and game in season can be obtained, but turkeys usually only at Christmas time. Fresh fruit and vegetables are not so abundant as in the United States, but there are generally some varieties all the year round. Frozen fruits and vegetables are stocked by most of the larger stores. Dried fruits, particularly raisins, are comparatively scarce and most grocery stores operate their own rationing scheme to ensure fair shares. Breakfast and cooking cereals present no difficulty.

Canned foods – meat, fish, fruits, soups, etc. – are available, but not of such quality and in such variety as in the United States.

For babies, high quality powdered milks and pasteurised tuberculin tested fresh milk are available. Recommended for the food parcel, however, are bottled Junior foods for children of 15 months and over.

Shopping conditions are rather different from those in the United States. Ordinarily, in the typical suburban shopping centre there are separate shops for bread and confectionery, meat, milk, vegetables, groceries, etc. – rarely are they all under one roof. Self-service and automatic vending do not yet approach such proportions as in the United States; none-the-less, self-service in particular, is becoming popular in Britain. Milk and bread are delivered daily. (The bread will usually be unwrapped unless it is sliced). It is most usual these days for the housewife to take delivery of other food items at the shops, but regular deliveries can be obtained without much difficulty.

**Clothing**: It will be found that all clothing, as well as household linen, etc., can be purchased in graded utility quality. The small CC tab or stamp indicates that the item is free of purchase tax and that the price is controlled. Utility goods, particularly clothes, must conform to a certain specification and are often of good value, especially "top grade" utility. The word "Utility" does not do justice to some of the excellent coats, suits, dresses, etc, sold under this controlled price scheme.

**For Ladies**: Suits, with blouses or jumpers are worn all the year round, as are casual skirts with blouses, cardigans and twin sets. Woollen dresses are worn for business and home during the winter and also during cooler summer days. Cotton and silk frocks are part of any summer wardrobe, when they are worn with a light coat if necessary. The most practical and popular wear is the suit for most informal occasions, with a top coat for winter wear.

With a live hat industry, latest Paris styles are quickly copied both as expensive and inexpensive models at smaller shops and departmental stores.

Shoes are in fair supply and styles are varied. Purchase tax exemption, under the Utility scheme, also applies to shoes.

Underwear is also quite plentiful, and simple garments can be purchased at reasonable prices. There is a fair supply of nylon lingerie now on the market, but it is rather expensive as against the usual silks, rayons, etc.

Good stockings are not so easy to come by. Pure silk is expensive and scarce; nylons are also scarce and mostly not nearly so sheer as the American variety.

It is, in fact, recommended that women bring all the nylon articles they are likely to require.

Fur coats, which carry purchase tax, are of course, very costly, although there is a range of utility furs to be had.

Evening wear follows the American and Paris styles closely. In London, particularly the West End, good and stylish evening and semi-evening wear can be found to suit most purses.

**For Men**: Men in Britain dress conservatively, particularly so far as colour is concerned. Ties, for instance, are not usually so colourful or expansive. Except in really hot weather (and then only on sports and recreative occasions) the menfolk stick rather rigidly to their jackets, collars and ties, and shirts are seldom worn outside the trouser belts.

Lounge suits differ little from the American style, except that the cut is not quite so loose in an English tailored suit. All shades of grey, navy, brown and also black are usually worn, but good suiting is not plentiful and well-tailored suits are expensive.

Shirts are obtainable with separate collars (usually semi-stiff) or with collar attached, although the latter are more often only available in sports shirts. It is possible to buy shirts on the American coat style. Striped or plain white shirts are most general wear; plain white, with stiff collars being quite popular for business or fairly formal occasions. At the moment, variety and supply are not of the best and prices may appear expensive by American standards.

Although coloured and patterned socks in wool, wool mixture and cotton are available, to the American the choice will probably appear limited. For general wear with lounge suits and for business wear particularly, men seem to prefer a fairly sober patterned or even plain sock.

Locknit underwear is in good supply, although pure wool is rather expensive. It is not easy to obtain the American type of cotton under-pants, however.

The most popular headgear – soft felt "trilby" hats usually have smaller brims than those worn in the United States.

**For Children**: Clothing for children may be obtained as easily in Britain as in America – excepting, possibly, clothes for boys up to the age of five years.

Diaper-washing services are generally not available.

**Dressing**: Generally, formal evening dress (white ties for men) is now only worn on very important occasions generally. First class restaurants and night clubs in London's West End often require evening clothes, but dinner jackets are more usually worn than tails. On the whole the war years have left behind a casual attitude towards dressing in the evening and the necessity for evening clothes will be rare.

Before you have been long in Britain you will want to know how much things cost. How much you will have to pay for commodities and how much butter, cheese, bacon and meat your rations will allow you. You will want to know how our cost of living compares with the American. This four-page supplement has been prepared to answer those questions and to give you some idea of current prices. It should be remembered that rationing fluctuates slightly and that all prices are rising. However, as a generalisation you will find that setting up a home costs about as much as in the States, but that living expenses are not so great. **)**

---

### Household ration per year in S.E. England

| | | *from* | | | *from* |
|---|---|---|---|---|---|
| Coal | 34 cwt | 5s 7d cwt (cwt = 112 lbs) | Coke | as available | 5s 5d cwt |

### Other Items (unrationed)

| | | | | |
|---|---|---|---|---|
| Bread | 6d (large loaf – just under 2 lbs) | | Motor spirit | 3s 8d gallon (1 Imperial gallon – 1.2 American) |
| Milk | | 6d pint | | |
| Coffee | | *from* 5s 0d lb | Pipe tobacco | from 4s 0d oz |
| Cigarettes | | *from* 3s 8d for 20 | | |

### Equivalents

£1 (one pound) = 2.80 dollars  
1s (one shilling) = 14 cents  

1d (one penny) = 1 cent (approx)

### Accommodation

| | *from* | | *from* |
|---|---|---|---|
| Houses to buy with vacant possession | £2,500 | Houses to rent (furnished) | £9 a week |
| Board residence, private houses | £5 a week | Apartments to rent (furnished) | £7 a week |
| Board residence, hotels | £8 a week | | |

### Domestic Help

| | | | |
|---|---|---|---|
| General help, living in | *from* £3 a week, plus board | Daily help | 3s per hour |

### Furniture and Household Goods

| | | | |
|---|---|---|---|
| Dining room suite | £75 | Gas washing machine | £40 |
| Lounge suite | £80 | Electric washing machine | £100 |
| Bedroom suite | £85 | Radio (table model) | £30 |
| Carpet (square or centre) | £30 | (licence required – £1 a from any Post Office) | |
| Carpet (fitted) | £80 | | |
| Cooker | £30 | Radiogram (licence as above) | £70 |
| Electric refrigerator | £120 | Television | £75 |
| Gas refrigerator | £70 | (licence required, £2 a year for radio and television) | |
| | | Hire of radio | *from* 5s a week |
| | | Hire of television | *from* 15s a week |

### THESE GOODS ARE RATIONED

| | | | | |
|---|---|---|---|---|
| | Beef | | 2s 6d lb | |
| | Lamb | (Individual ration to | 2s 6d lb | (Average price |
| Meat | Pork | value of 1s 7d per week) | 2s 6d lb | according to cut) |
| | Veal | | 2s 0d lb | |

### Individual ration per week

| | | | | | |
|---|---|---|---|---|---|
| Butter | 3 ozs | 2s 6d a lb | Bacon | 3 ozs | *from* 2s 11d a lb |
| Sugar | 10 ozs | 6d a lb | Margarine | 4 ozs | 1s 2d a lb |
| Candy | 6 ozs | *from* 3s 0d a lb | Lard (cooking fat) | 4 ozs | 1s 4d a lb |
| Cheese | 2 ozs | *from* 2s 0d a lb | Tea | 2 ozs | *from* 3s 8d a lb |

*1917: King George V visits troops at Vimy Ridge in a Vauxhall. The staff car had gone through the Flanders mud "as far as a car could go!"*

*General (later Field Marshal) Edmund Allenby, leader of the Egyptian Expeditionary Force, making a triumphal entry into Jerusalem after defeating the Turkish army. The car is a 25 hp staff car.*

*HM George VI inspects one of the first Churchill tanks to leave the production line in June 1941. Charles Bartlett, Director of Vauxhall Motors, is on the left of the picture. The tanks were tested in the grounds of Luton Hoo, the country seat of the Wernher family.*

*One of the 5,640 38-ton Churchill tanks and one of 100 or so 10 hp cars built for government use. One of these tanks was offered to Vauxhall's Heritage collection some years ago but unfortunately had to be declined.*

*A square-faced 15 cwt Bedford pickup known to all ex-servicemen disembarks from a beach landing craft.*

*A Bedford QL in the North African desert. The 4-wheel drive QL was Bedford's first foray into this 4 x 4 field. The QL became the ancestor of a line of military-type cross-country trucks that continued until the 1980s, with sales to armies of several countries, including of course the British Army.*

*During the war the Vauxhall Motors' orchestra held a number of concerts to help the war effort. This picture was taken in 1943 outside a camouflaged Luton Town Hall. By 1945 the Luton branch of National Savings had raised an incredible £15 million and the orchestra had certainly played some part in that success.*

# Employees and Managing Directors

Many people have contributed to the success of Vauxhall Motors and to include everyone would mean that this book would extend to several volumes. I have therefore selected a sample of staff and Managing Directors who have appeared in local newspapers.

### John Barber

Former apprentice John Barber has risen through the ranks to become Director of Manufacturing at the Luton plant where 4,000 people are employed. He was educated at Dunstable Grammar School and went on to become a student apprentice at the Luton College of Technology (now Luton University) before joining Vauxhall after obtaining his Higher National Diploma. His first job at Vauxhall was in time study. After various production assignments at Luton, in 1965 he went to Ellesmere Port as a general foreman to help set up the new body shop there. For the next 19 years he had a number of senior appointments in production management until he became Quality Control Manager. In 1984 he returned to Luton as Plant Manager and was appointed Manufacturing Director in January 1988. Since April 1990 he has been on the Board of Directors.

### Charles Bartlett

Bartlett was born in Bibury, Gloucestershire, in 1889. He attended the village school and completed his education at Bath Technical College where he trained in business methods and accounts. After the First World War he joined General Motors as an accounting clerk at its London branch in Hendon. Promotion was rapid and in 1926 he was appointed Managing Director.

In 1930 Bartlett was promoted to the position of Managing Director at the enlarged Vauxhall works in Luton. The story goes that he was chosen for this important job because General Motors wanted an Englishman to run Vauxhall. A director of General Motors on being asked to provide a suitable candidate is quoted as saying: "Well I guess it had better be Charlie Bartlett; he's about as English as they come." At the time General Motors was aware of the economic nationalism within the British motor vehicle market and was keen to have an all-British product made by British workers with a British managing director at the helm.

Bartlett had a broad-based intellect and a colleague says he was "a determined character (with) a strong stocky physique and a sense of humour that leavened what could otherwise have been too paternal an outlook towards the Vauxhall workforce". He was constantly walking around the factory and offices, making a habit of talking to employees.

He fostered a father and son system of recruitment whereby company employees tended to have greater opportunity in placing their sons in positions of apprenticeship than a mere outsider. This unofficial system became known as the "Vauxhall Family". Everyone became a company "Ambassador", a keen salesman of the company's name and products with the result that they tended to work much harder than in many other companies.

Bartlett introduced a profit-sharing scheme for the workers and developed the group bonus system. He also set up the Management Advisory Committee whose purpose was to enable grievances among the workers to be dealt with by a committee made up of management, foremen and shop floor workers. During Bartlett's period as managing director there were no serious industrial disputes at Vauxhall. Under Bartlett's control the first car to roll off the assembly line in 1930 was the Vauxhall Cadet. The smaller and more popular Vauxhall Ten followed in 1935. Bartlett convinced General Motors that a truck was the best thing for Vauxhall. This proved to be a life saver for the company and production in the light truck market, which was 11,200 in 1931, rose to a commercial vehicle output of 60,800 by 1954.

Bartlett was knighted in 1944 for his own and his company's outstanding contribution to the war effort. He continued as managing director until he became Chairman of Vauxhall in June 1953, a post he occupied until he retired at the end of the following year. He died in August 1955 aged 65.

### Peter Batchelor

Mr Batchelor joined the company as an apprentice at AC Delco in Dunstable in 1954. He qualified as a chartered engineer before taking up a number of appointments in AC Delco's automotive equipment sales. He transferred to Vauxhall in 1982. He progressed through several senior positions before becoming Vice-Chairman, Commercial Operations, in 1993. In April 1994 he took early retirement.

### Robert Boylen

Mr Boylen was a former Luton Town footballer who played 11 games as a right-winger for the Hatters between 1928 and 1930 before transferring to Gillingham. After finishing his professional career, he worked for 40 years at Vauxhall and regularly turned out for the firm's South Midlands League team. He died in 1992 aged 85.

### William Ebbert

Mr Ebbert began his GM career as a graduate trainee with its Terex Division in Hudson, Ohio, moving up through various finance jobs with Terex and at GM's main office in Detroit. In 1977 he became Assistant Controller at AC Spark Plug and five years later went to Saginaw Steering Gear progressing through several senior jobs before moving to Troy, Michigan, working for the Automotive Components Group as Director, Business Operations. In September 1991 he joined Vauxhall and was Chairman and Managing Director until June 1993 when he was promoted to the new position of President, General Motors Automotive Components Group, Asia-Pacific Operations, based in Tokyo.

### Tom Forder

Tom joined Vauxhall Motors in 1980 in the export boxing department. In 1993 he was awarded the British Empire Medal for his charity work. This started in 1984 when his own children needed hospital treatment. The first charity event was a five-a-side football competition in Vauxhall's trim shop, where he currently works on door-latch fitting. The AC Trim Charity Appeal was later formed and has now raised more than £13,000. Initially the fund was for Luton and Dunstable Hospital children's department but funds have also been given to Great Ormond Street Hospital and other worthy causes.

### Eric Fountain

Mr Fountain spent nearly 46 years at Vauxhall starting as a 14-year-old office boy. He progressed to become a planning engineer before becoming the Plant Manager at Bedford Trucks, Dunstable, in 1970. He became a main board director of Vauxhall and the Manager at Ellesmere Port in 1974. The following year he was appointed as Director of Manufacturing at

Luton, Dunstable, Ellesmere Port and Antwerp. In 1981 until his retirement in 1989 he was Director of Public Affairs. He was awarded the OBE in 1986 for services to the motor industry and community.

In December 1994 he was appointed the new Chairman of Luton and Dunstable Hospital NHS Trust. A former High Sheriff of Bedfordshire, Mr Fountain is Director of Bedfordshire TEC, trustee of Luton and South Beds Hospice and County Vice President of St John Ambulance.

### Charles Golden

Charles Golden took over as Chairman and Managing Director of Vauxhall Motors on June 1 1993. A native of Fort Wayne, Indiana, Mr Golden began his career with GM in New York in 1970. His first job was as an analyst in the treasurer's office from where he progressed to various management positions within the corporation. In 1989 he became treasurer and was promoted to Vice President in November 1992, a few months before coming to Luton. He made his home in north London with his wife and two children. In March 1996 he announced that he was quitting the company for an executive post with a giant American drugs company.

### Geoffrey Moore, CBE

Mr Moore was born in Dunstable in 1916 and joined Vauxhall's Finance Department in 1933. On the outbreak of the Second World War he was commissioned into the Royal Army Service Corps and served in the Far East from 1941, where he was taken prisoner by the Japanese at the fall of Singapore.

Upon his return to Vauxhall in 1946 he moved up through the Sales Department, joining the Board as Sales Director in 1967. In 1979 he was appointed Chairman. He retired in 1981.

When Mr Moore died in 1989, the Chairman and Managing Director of Vauxhall said: "We are all saddened by the news. Geoffrey Moore made an important contribution to the development of Vauxhall and was widely respected for his extensive involvement in both industry and the community."

### Ken Parks

Ken Parks celebrated 50 years of service with Vauxhall in 1994. The maintenance engineer started work at the Luton plant as a boy of 14, when Britain was still at war and Vauxhall were making Churchill tanks and army lorries.

### James Reginald Pearson

Reg Pearson was born in 1897 in Dudley. After leaving school at 15 he continued with evening classes at a local technical college. In 1913 he started a machining apprenticeship with the firm of Bullers Ltd of Tipton. Then came a brief spell in the Royal Flying Corps followed by training at the National Projectile factory in the Black Country.

In 1919 Pearson travelled to Luton hoping to be employed with a local machine tool company. However, when he arrived the vacancy had been filled so he applied for a job at Vauxhall. He started work with Vauxhall in September 1919 as a centre-lathe turner in the machine shop.

In 1927 he became a foreman. The then managing director, Charles Bartlett, had a policy of promoting shop floor workers to managerial positions. Two years later Pearson was made an area manager and in 1934 he became Assistant Production Manager. In 1939 he became Production Manager and was heavily involved in the changeover to war-time production of Bedford trucks and later Churchill tanks. In 1942 he became Factory Manager. Despite the factory being damaged twice by enemy bombers, Pearson kept the plant in full production.

In 1946 Pearson was appointed a director of Vauxhall Motors and in 1950 he was awarded the OBE. In 1953 he was appointed Executive Assistant to the Managing Director and in 1958 he became a Deputy Chairman of the Board of Directors. In 1959 he was knighted for his immense contribution to the British motor industry, in peace and war. He retired from Vauxhall Motors in December 1962.

### Maurice Platt

Mr Platt joined Vauxhall in July 1937 just as the H-type Vauxhall Ten went into production. He became Chief Engineer and before his retirement in 1963, he was responsible for the Victor and Viva ranges. He also developed the company's Bedford lorries and vans. He died in 1993 on his 95th birthday.

### Laurence H. Pomeroy

Born in 1883 Pomeroy became one of the most distinguished and respected British designers. Before working for Vauxhall he served an apprenticeship with the North London Railway Co. Pomeroy joined Vauxhall and became its designer. In 1908, at the age of 25, he had designed a car that "put Vauxhall in the forefront of advanced thinking". Two years later he was "coaxing 100 mph out of Vauxhall sports cars at Brooklands" and in 1912 he became Vauxhall's Chief Designer.

After the war Pomeroy decided that he wanted to move on. The inventor Lanchester, who was a consultant to Daimler, wrote: "If I had shares in Vauxhall I would sell them quick. It was as nearly a one-man show as anything in the country!" Pomeroy left Vauxhall to go to the United States where he built an all-aluminium car.

He returned from America to join Daimler. In 1936 he decided to leave the car industry and went to de Havilland Aircraft as general manager of their engine division.

He later moved on to H.M. Hobson. He died in 1941.

### Paul Tosch

Mr Tosch, an engineer who joined GM in 1958, came to the UK in 1986. During his time at Vauxhall Paul Tosch was that "quiet American who got on with the job and achieved a good deal. He did what GM told him to, but he did it in reasonable style. He has been one of the best MDs we've had and we were very impressed."

Boss of Bedford commercial vehicles from 1986, he found a new answer for Bedford after a merger with Leyland was blocked by the government. The solution was the sale of the Dunstable truck side to AWD in 1987 and the Luton van factory merged successfully with Japanese firm Isuzu to form IBCV.

Mr Tosch moved over to Vauxhall in November 1987 and saw the firm make four successive years of profits, with output and market share leaping ahead before he left Luton in September 1991 for a new job with GM's Harrison Component division.

### Peter Vigor

Peter was one of the best-known names in Vauxhall through his 33-year association with the *Mirror* before his retirement in 1975.

He started as a compositor and stonehand at the *Luton News* but during the war local papers were forced to contract which meant that Peter had to find another job. Vauxhall needed labour so he went to work on the line at the factory making tanks and trucks.

Peter loved writing so he submitted one or two articles to the Vauxhall magazine, the *Mirror.* The editor, Richard Hopkins, invited Peter to join the magazine and when Richard was promoted up the management ladder Peter became Editor, a job that was to last 30 years.

# Board of Directors

## as at June 1, 1974

**W. R. Price**
Chairman and
Managing Director

**J. H. Alden, CBE**
Environmental
Activities Staff

**H. A. Clark**
Sales

**A. A. Cunningham**
European Operations,
General Motors
Overseas Corporation

**E. D. Fountain**
Plant Manager,
Ellesmere Port plant

**J. R. Hebden**
Treasurer

**R. R. Hopkins, CBE**
Personnel

**W. B. Larson**
Chief Engineer

**D. C. Lowe**
Manufacturing

**G. E. Moore**
Government and Public
Relations

**P. G. H. Newton**
General Motors
Overseas Corporation

**C. F. P. Waller**
Supply

**L. W. Wright**
Reliability and Quality
Control

Staff of lacquering shop, 1916. Mrs Nellie Burley is in the middle of the first row. Also in the picture is foreman Bill Smith, who later took over a garage in Stuart Street. Mrs Burley was 16 when the photograph was taken. She worked at Vauxhall as a material handler during the whole of the First World War and then was employed in a number of local hat factories. During part of the Second World War she again worked as a material handler.

The sombre faces of the workers in the above picture contrast strongly with the smiling Vauxhall employees seen below who are saying that they are "fit for work".

*The year is 1935 and the only women employees, except a few employed on inspection work, are to be found operating these rapid-moving powerful sewing or trim machines.*

*Employees of Plant maintenance and Project blocks Y and Z, about 1945. Back Row: Reg White (fifth from left). Front Row: Mr Girdlestone, Charles Archer, Alf Sargent, Mac Smith and Ernie Nicholls. Others include Jimmy Launders, Jim Smith, "Jimmy" King, Tom Unstead and R H Bygrave.*

*The comptometer section of the Luton cost office, April 25 1961. Pictured, left to right, are (front row) Dorothy Linsdell and Mary Phillips; (second row) Hazel Battams, Yvonne Buckingham, Pat Whitworth; (third row) Gillian Davis, Joan Collins, Pearl Kilmister; (fourth row) Beryl Smith, Mary Stobbs, Jean Richardson; (fifth row) Eileen Telford, Doris Chlad, Joyce Parker; (sixth row) Christine Walker, and standing on either side of the supervisor Marion Hawkins are Rosemary Thompson and (next to window) Marion Buddon. Marion Hawkins was the supervisor for many years.*

*George Brown, Bill Staples, Fred Howlett and Ron Meers with a Vernons Pools cheque for £87,879.75. They were part of a seven-strong syndicate in Material and Production Control who each won over £12,000 in 1990.*

*Employees celebrate the Cavalier back as the number one best seller in the UK, February 1990. Pictured are Sharon Leon, Brian Groom, Jim Davis, Gordon Mead, Chris Grzesczuk, Pam Hopkins, Shirley Batchelor, Wally Lupton, Max Cooper and Geoff Willmott.*

*In December 1990 commemorative presentations were made by Paul Tosch to the following 25-year employees, most of whom are pictured above: R. Bastable, C. Common, J. D. Barrett, R. M. Brewer, A. R. Currington, J. Hurst, E. Manton, J. M. Nutkins, J. P. Roberts, P. D. F. Sterne, V. F. Shepherd, M. C. Pressland, T. M. Pearce, T. E. Carlisle, R. C. Dale, T. P. Dobbyn, R. S. Pepper, K. Patel, B. J. Brown, C. J. Gordon, T. J. Jones.*

*Every item of specification added to Vauxhall cars at Luton and Ellesmere Port results from a plan produced in Griffin House. Specification includes colour and trim of vehicles, car badges, seat belts, and even the glove box light. Decisions are based on market research and cost. The team suggests to Opel and GM's European designers what should be included in the British models. Pictured are the Product Planners in 1991: Ernie Hooper, John Winter, Wendy Grey, Phil Harwood, John Rutherford, Martin Lay, Paul Confrey, Stuart Harris.*

*Dave Hall (centre) and colleagues Roy Adams and John Beal with their fire vehicles and the Vauxhall ambulance. They are part of the Luton Fire and Security Department. The fire unit deals with some 1,300 calls a year, from both within and outside the plant. During the summer they have an average of two grass fires a day on the nearby railway tracks which jeopardize Vauxhall property on the south side of Kimpton Road.*

*Tom Reilly won £130 under the Employee Recognition Scheme for his idea to reduce the size of paint pots he uses. Only a tiny amount of paint was needed each week. Previously this paint was held in large pots which cost more than a pound each, and in which the paint went hard quickly and had to be thrown away. Tom is pictured in July 1991 with the old, large bottles and the new tiny ones.*

*Luton Mayor Cllr Ray Sills opens Vauxhall's Heritage Centre in May 1993. With him are company director Tony Burnip, Tony Spalding and Vauxhall's oldest living former employee, Lewy Norris, 98. Lutonian Lewy Norris started work at the car plant in 1915, just ten years after the factory opened. A former commercial department employee, he signed the company's first £1 million cheque to the government during his 44 years with the firm.*

*Paul Tosch, former Chairman and Managing Director.*

*Charles Golden, who was Chairman and Managing Director from 1993 to 1996.*

# Social and Sporting Activities

Charles Bartlett, who was Managing Director from 1930, followed a policy of promoting men to positions of responsibility from off the shop floor. Bartlett saw social and sporting activities as an important way of demonstrating the skills necessary for management. He helped promote drama and sporting facilities. Peter Vigor recalls in an interview with Len Holden: "If you wanted to get on with Bartlett you had to take an interest in the Recreation Club. For example you might take up tennis and sit on the Tennis Club Committee and become chairman. This showed Bartlett that you could organise." The Vauxhall Recreation Club used to have some 30 sections which included everything from minor hobbies to sport and horticulture. Many activities took place in the huge canteen which fronted Kimpton Road. Peter Vigor recalled his own personal record for the *Luton News* Vauxhall Souvenir Supplement:

‘The canteen was not a beautiful building, although the steps at the front and the facade were impressive. It was constructed like a huge aeroplane hangar. At the time it was built it was considered a colossus, but it was soon too small for the company's requirements and a further large two-storey extension was stuck on the end of it.

Whereas the original roof was 40 feet or so high, with plenty of skylights, the addition was only 15 feet high, with no roof windows, its ceiling being the floor of the weekly-paid staff canteen, which was transformed into a ballroom or what was called the Vauxhall Theatre when the occasions arose.

Under the extension it was often dark, dungeon-like. It probably spoiled the architect's sense of proportion. It certainly did not add to the beauty of the interior.

There were other canteens in this complex: the hourly-paid and weekly-paid (which included monthly), the directors' dining room and the management group dining room.

The kitchens, serveries and offices were extensive as there were three meal-breaks a day for the day shift and three for the night shift. I estimate well over 10,000 meals a day were served when the factory was working full out, not counting snacks at breakfast and tea times.

The bar room included six billiards tables, dart boards and an indoor skittles alley, and committee rooms and a shop.

There was a fully-equipped stage with dressing rooms, and showers that could be used at any time. Badminton and table tennis sections of the Rec Club were regular users, but they were available to anyone who worked in the company.

When it was demolished it was not so much the heaps of bricks and mortar which saddened me, but the thoughts and memories that went through my head.

During the war I used the main canteen for my meals and snacks. The food was of high quality and the kitchens spotless. Food rationing never bothered me because five or six days a week I had my main meal in the canteen.

I also enjoyed monthly dances, table tennis, badminton and boxing shows there. At Christmas and on sports days the canteen was decorated and used for the celebrations. Those occasions were quite a sight, something like the Tower Ballroom at Blackpool!

The staff canteen ballroom floor was sprung maple, and Sir Reginald Pearson, president of the rec club and of the social section, was very proud of this floor, and had it protected with a heavy canvas drugget. He threatened dire consequences if he found anyone dropped a cigarette end on this covering or on the floor. To think that a demolition firm swung a concrete dolly over this floor and dropped it time and time again until the maple was mere firewood to be burned on site . . . sacrilege!

Another feature of this great clumsy building was the four or five murals behind the serveries in the hourly-paid canteen.

These were painted during the war by a woman artist commissioned by the rec club through David Jones, the styling manager. I understand someone took a picture before they too were demolished. The murals depicted the fishing industry, harvesting and other scenes reminiscent of the food chain. I loved those paintings, not because I thought them masterpieces but because there among the clamour of cups and cutlery rattling on enamel-topped tables, and queues of boiler-suited workers, they reminded me of fresh air and the peaceful countryside.

I doubt if many Vauxhallite memories are of art, or peace and quiet in the main canteen. And yet . . . what about the symphony concerts, when the London Philharmonic Orchestra under Sir Adrian Boult and other mainline conductors filled the canteen to capacity? Hard chairs cost a shilling (5p) and there were a few armchairs at 2s 6d (12.5p). Nobody grumbled about the seating.

But the noise of the crickets, the draughts and the distance from the town centre of Luton finally made the Vauxhall music section move to the more comfortable seating arrangements at local cinemas, like the Alma, Odeon and Savoy.

There was home-produced music too, for Fred W. Green organised Sunday concerts with stars from the London variety theatres. The male voice choir and the girls choir joined the Vauxhall Concert Orchestra, and then the big stage had to be extended by an apron to accommodate the whole cast.

Theatrical shows in the staff canteen drew large audiences. The average was three shows a year, farce, comedy or drama, including a production of Shakespeare's Taming of the Shrew.

Each Christmas there were two or three children's parties, with employees volun-teering for all kinds of duties, from clowning to marshalling the hundreds of noisy and rumbustious youngsters. I remember when Sir Reginald Pearson took off his coat to load the children on to a log slide. In later years children demanded more sophisticated entertainment, and were taken to pantomimes, at Oxford and London.

One of my earliest memories of the canteen was the flower, fruit and vegetables piled almost to the ceiling for shows of the horticultural section and supported by Messrs Andrews, landscape gardeners of Leagrave.

And the art exhibitions – 500 pictures by employees from all departments, and once including five by managing director Sir William Swallow. Photographic exhibitions, badminton and table tennis tournaments, brass band competitions . . . sometimes these events were so popular they almost took over the canteen for a weekend.

There was even a dog show, which was banned after only one year because Arthur Adams, the canteen manager, objected to it on hygienic grounds.

Sometimes the company used the main canteen for long-service gold watch presentations, management group meetings, presentations for safety, savings and accident-free driving. There were huge dinners for the 25-year club.

In the general council room all the larger club committees met, under photographs of Sir Charles Bartlett and Sir Reginald Pearson. They had been keen supporters of the recreation club, and both were Presidents.

The pensioners used this room for business meetings, and the staff canteen for monthly social evenings.

Sometimes the canteen was too popular. Sparrows loved the warmth and the crumbs. The management tried many means to get rid of them – owls, bird lime and traps among them.

But like me they were enthusiasts. They got far more out of Vauxhall Motors than just scratching a living.**,**

*The cavernous canteen in Kimpton Road, 1930s. There used to be three lunch sittings and a bar. No one thought it strange for employees to have a couple of pints at lunch-time. Today the canteen has been demolished. There are no lunch breaks for the production departments because they are on double-day shift. No one drinks during working hours any more.*

*One Saturday afternoon in January 1949 saw the canteen hosting three consecutive employees' children's parties. This is party number two and each youngster in neatly labelled.*

*A fleet of buses ferried nearly 1,000 children of Vauxhall employees who went to see the pantomime* Cinderella *starring Roy Castle, at the New Theatre, Oxford, in January 1970.*

## Concert Band

Vauxhall Concert Orchestra was formed in February 1934 when six members of the gear machine shop decided to form a works band. They met on Sundays for rehearsals. One of the original six members was Ted Willis who was 84 in 1994. The orchestra poached Fred Green from Jacksons of Dallow Road and he became its conductor.

The orchestra flourished, performing every week in the canteen and at outside venues. During the war its fund-raising concerts helped Luton save an outstanding £15 million for National Savings.

After the war its concerts attracted top variety stars such as Jerry Allen, Max Miller, Gracie Fields (in 1943), Ten-Ton Tessie O'Shea and the conductor Sir Adrian Boult. On one occasion the Andrews Family performed, with six-year-old Julie, who later became the star of My Fair Lady and Mary Poppins, playing the trumpet.

In 1964, following the death of Fred Green, Denis Hyde the lead trumpeter for many years, took over as conductor.

The band used to give no fewer than nine Christmas concerts when General Motors' local empire included AC Delco, Bedford Trucks and Toddington Road. The band travelled far and wide with its music.

By the end of 1980 the orchestra had changed to a wind band and the name changed from Vauxhall Motors Concert Orchestra to the Vauxhall Motors Concert Band. It continued to travel widely and in 1990 the band gained the title of Home Counties Champions and played in the finals of the National Concert Band Festival in Manchester. The band held its Diamond Jubilee concert in 1994 and around a quarter of the young 50-strong band work for Vauxhall.

*Fred Green, who died in 1964, was founder of the Vauxhall Concert Orchestra. He was its musical director for 26 years. He was also musical director of the Vauxhall Girls' Choir and was a vice-president of the Vauxhall Male Voice Choir.*

*Peter Jenkins is the current musical director of the Vauxhall Concert Band. Although Peter is primarily a science teacher, after establishing Icknield High School Band he became the conductor of Vauxhall Concert Band in 1982.*

*Vauxhall Orchestra, Christmas 1942. The sign at the back reads "May 1943 Bring Victory".*

*The orchestra travelled far and wide to give concerts. Some of the most notable were at Walthamstow for several years in the 1950s, the Manor House Hospital, London, for their summer fete and at St Dunstan's for the blind. Concerts were held locally in church halls and in Wardown Park, which is still used as a venue today.*

*Male Voice Choir, 1967. Back row, left to right: A. Lake, A. D. Jones, W. Davies, T. Price, G. Roberts, B. Davies, W. Daniel, D. McKelvey, C. Wheeler, R. Crisp, A. Burr, W. Brown, J. Ratcliffe. Second row: J. Dolan, A. Haines, R. Boyd, M. Lowrie, J. Worthing, G. Evans, A. Boughey, B. Hopkins. Third row: W. Prodger, E. Barry, G. Foster, W. Laverty, F. Lowndes, W. Owens, F. Bricknell, H. Crow. Fourth row: T. Hopkins, T. Owens, A. Lyons, E. Clarke, P. Richardson, B. Tyler, T. Roberts, T. Burton. Front row: Vice-Presidents C. F. Davidson, J. Manton, Denis Hyde, Accompanist Joan Lane, Musical Director Trevor Watkins, President C. Cooper, Chairman of Recreation Club W. Butt, and Vice-President A. Butterfield.*

*The Vauxhall Orchestra and Ladies Choir, 1976.*

The Winslow Boy *was performed for three nights by Vauxhall Motors theatrical section (now known as the Griffin Players) at the works canteen, October 1948. Producer Stan Moody can be seen here going over part of the script. The title role was taken by 14-year-old Dunstable Grammar School boy Robert Tuffnell and his father (right) by F. Smith-Peterson.*

*Vauxhall Male Voice Choir, formed in 1943, entertain guests of the Luton Old People's Welfare committee at the Town Hall, February 1954. One member at this time was Alf Lake.*

*Demonstration by members of the Vauxhall Judo Club to the boys and girls of Chapel Street Youth Club, March 1956.*

*The men's 100 yards "York" contest at Vauxhall's open archery shoot, August 1960. Competitors came from as far afield as Liverpool and Norwich.*

*Photographic section members on their annual outing to the Vale of Evesham, about 1964.*

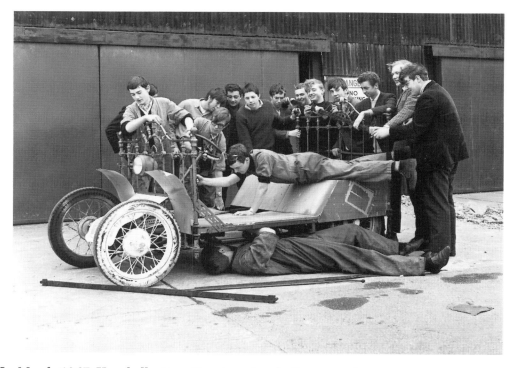

In March 1967 Vauxhall apprentices issued a challenge to other apprentice associations to take part in a bedstead-pushing race around Luton. The proposed rules of the six-mile race were that the bedsteads would be fitted with brakes and steering, probably from old car chassis! The castors were to be replaced by wheels. Five apprentices were to push the bed with two lying on it, operating the brakes and steering system. All contestants were to be in fancy dress. Prizes were to be awarded for the best decorated bed with the team in the most original costume as well as for the fastest bed pushers.

*Eleven finalists of the 1967 Miss Spectacular Contest, the winner of which had the privilege of officiating at the Vauxhall Spectacular Sports Day, together with Honor Blackman and Jackie Pallo. Seated: Linda Greenwood (2nd), Mrs Ruth Williams (Miss Spectacular), and Marion Moule (3rd). Standing: Mrs Lesley Sutton, Mrs Valerie Giles, Jean Lake, Sally Bedingfield, Diane Burnage, Denise Allen, Patricia Miller and Evelyn Wilson.*

*Apprentices' children's party, Short Pavilion, Brache Estate, December 1969. Among those present were five-year-old Claire McMullen and 17-year-old Linda Currie.*

*Opening of the new track of the Model Car Racing Club by W. C. Butt, Chairman of the Recreation Club, February 1970. The six-track 140 ft lane was designed and made by club members at a cost of £1,500. The cars, which were also made by members, were capable of speeds of 50 mph. Watching the model cars are Keith Hall (reigning champion), Mr Butt, Dr K. Pocock (chairman of the section and vice-chairman of the Recreation Club), Frank Ford (vice-chairman of the section), Mick Robinson and Gordon Sibley.*

*Paul Orme, 20-year-old Luton apprentice, was among the runners-up in the 1970 Vauxhall Craftsman's Guild competition in which more than 600 entrants submitted designs for a "Car of the Future". Paul designed a four-seater sports saloon to take a four-rotor Wankel engine, and it took him 400 hours to build the model in fibreglass. David Hegland, Vauxhall's Managing Director, is pictured inspecting Paul's car.*

*Six pretty semi-finalists of the 1970 "Miss Vauxhall" competition. Pictured are Glenise Woolhouse, Brenda Owen, Lorraine Wildman, Marie Richard, Janet Yates and Esther Hornsby. These six appeared at the Vauxhall Spectacular Sports Day in June when the winner was chosen by celebrity guests, disc jockey Tony Blackburn, comedian Dick Emery and his TV wife, Josephine Blake.*

*The girls from the sales department hold a hen party, their first annual Christmas dinner at Hexton, 1964.*

*The Dunstable Annual Christmas party, 1964. William Swallow, M. A. Aldridge, A. F. King, C. F. Davidson, A. Bourn, N. Maskell and their wives were amongst the merrymakers. Music was provided by the Ramblers Orchestra and the MC was Keith Mayles.*

*Pensioners' Annual Christmas party at Luton on December 4 1990. Six hundred pensioners and their wives attended the annual event making it a complete sell-out.*

*Enjoying a laugh: Barbara Row, Kathleen Essex, Works Manager David Cato, Sylvia Curtis, Neil Gardner, Shirley Batchelor and Alec Curtis, Christmas 1990.*

*Ted Read thanks Tony Lines, Personnel Manager, for the management team's hard work at the Pensioners' Christmas party, 1990. From left: Joy Young, Janet Lines, retired director David Young, Tony Lines, Ted and Olive Read.*

## Sporting Activities

*Athletic Club swimming section 1916-17 (above) and Athletic Club football team, 1918-19 (below).*

*Vauxhall football team, 1924.*

*Vauxhall Motors' football team which beat Peterborough in the FA Cup. They were the first Vauxhall team to reach the first round proper of the FA Cup. Pictured in November 1947 are, Back row: K. Andrews, R. Campbell, W. Weston. Centre row: K. Edge (secretary), A. Laing, W. Hare, G. Cosgrove, "Snowy" White (trainer). Front row: H. Marriott, K. Brazier, S. Smith, K. Chambers K. Sharp.*

*Men's 33-yard freestyle handicap, September 1948, Waller Street Baths, Luton.*

*Vauxhall "A" badminton team, November 1952. Pictured are, standing: L. Bandy, I. Offer,*
*T. Clark, G. Smith. Seated: Mrs L. Bass, Mrs H. Nye, Mrs J. Ivory, Mrs J. Bailey.*

*Vauxhall hockey team in quartered skirts go into attack against Welwyn Garden City in Vauxhall Motors' annual six-a-side ladies' hockey tournament, April 1953.*

*Rugby section pictured in April 1953. Rugby football had been introduced to Luton in about 1905 by a team formed by workers of the newly-arrived Vauxhall Works, who played on a pitch adjoining the factory.*

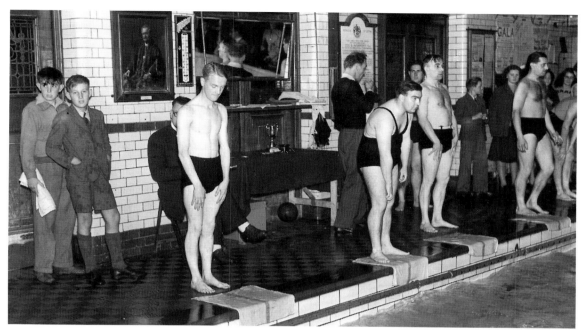

*Men's 100 yards freestyle final at Vauxhall Recreation Club's annual swimming gala held at the Waller Street Baths, Luton, September 1954.*

*Vauxhall netball captain Mrs M. Kindred receiving the Eileen Davis Challenge Cup from Mr A. R. Gulland, hon treasurer of the Commer Cars Ltd Sports Club, after the match with Dunstable Netball Club, April 1956.*

*In October 1959 the cricket club held its annual dinner at the Cresta Restaurant. Sir Reginald Pearson chats with Surrey County cricketer Tom Clark who was at one time a playing member of the Vauxhall club.*

*Vauxhall first eleven which won through to the first round proper of the Amateur Cup, 1967. Back row: J. Millar (press secretary), F. Weedon (assistant hon secretary), G. Cosgrove (trainer), D. Clark, D. Wiles, M. Casey (playing in place of D. Summers), D. Matthews, J. Fennell, F. Weedon, G. Turner (manager), R. Mailing, P. Yarnell (chairman). Front row: P. Cresale, J. Watt, S. Watt, D. Mardle (captain), G. Mullen, M. Hoar. Inset: D. Summers.*

*Winners of the Paint Shop five-a-side football league, "the Mad Cows". The victorious team, pictured in 1991, were Paul Daniel, Wayne Rideout, John Wood, Russell Clarke, Steve Crichton, Ian Cox, Dougal Martin and Paul Janes.*

# In the Community

Vauxhall has established close links with local charities, schools, hospital and industry. During 1994 the company supported 195 charities and organisations including the NSPCC, the Cancer Relief Macmillan Fund, the industry-run charity BEN – the Motor and Allied Trades Benevolent Fund – and the Scouting movement.

In 1994 Vauxhall stepped in to sponsor a new Cub Scout award – the Road Safety Badge. It is the first time a badge has been specially created for a sponsor. To earn the badge, Cub Scouts must identify ten traffic signs, show that they know how to use zebra, pelican and railway crossings, walk safely on a road with no footpath and make an emergency phone call. They must also demonstrate safe behaviour as a car passenger. Over 50,000 badges had been distributed by February 1995.

Christmas 1994 again saw Vauxhall supporting the Crisis Messiah concert in aid of the homeless which was held at St Paul's Church in Knightsbridge, London. The concert, which was broadcast by Classic FM, raised £30,000.

*A car push raises money for Children in Need, 1990. Luton plant director John Barber (front seat), presents Vauxhall's donation to Pepe Garcia and Les Jellis (back seat) as (left to right) Tracey McNaughton, Jason Mosedale and Steven Parsons look on.*

*Vauxhall Parts charity committee (above) helped raise £525 towards Natalie McConachie's Disneyland fund in December 1990. Natalie, aged two, had abnormally small kidneys and was not expected to live beyond 1991. Pictured (centre) is Dave Nixon, Manager of Vauxhall Parts, with Natalie and her mother and her grandmother, Wendy (right), surrounded by members of the Vauxhall Parts charity committee. The following April saw the charity committee (below) present a touch screen computer and motorized lawnmower to local charities.*

*Soft Trim bakers with their charity cakes, December 1990. They auctioned entries in a cake competition raising more than £200 for local charities.*

*The annual Vauxhall Motors' sponsored Christmas extravaganza* Joy to the World *was a glittering success in 1990. The show at the Royal Albert Hall was in aid of the Save the Children Fund and other children's charities. Pictured with Princess Margaret are Chairman and Managing Director Paul Tosch, his fiancee Gay Gilezean, Executive Director of Sales and Marketing Peter Batchelor and his wife Gill.*

*A donation of £100,000 by Vauxhall paid for a floor of sheltered housing in a wing named after Vauxhall at Town Thorns, the motor industry benevolent fund's (BEN) latest centre. The charity already offers permanent care to a total of 37 Vauxhall employees and former employees. Representing Vauxhall at the opening in 1991 were, left to right: Colin Bithell, John Fetherstone, Tony Room, George Davis, Managing Director and Chief Executive Paul Tosch (second from right) and Ken Davies (extreme right). Geoffrey Atkinson and Christine Watton of BEN are pictured centre.*

# Dealers, Publicity and Sales

Initially the majority of Vauxhall customers purchased their car from the original factory in London and then, after the company moved in 1905, they bought from the Luton factory, where closer attention could be given to their individual requirements. However, as sales expanded, particularly from 1908 onwards, this became increasingly more difficult.

Cars were also sold from Vauxhall's London office at Leadenhall Street. This doubled as an office for its marine engines as well. In 1912 the company acquired showrooms in Great Portland Street which in 1919 were handed over to its agents, Messrs Shaw & Kilburn Limited. Other dealers were appointed (with the result that today Vauxhall has around 510 retailers) and this enabled Vauxhall to concentrate on the production of its cars. In 1995 the dealers became known as retailers. The new name arose because they were now into retailing rather than dealing as in the old days.

Exhibitions in the form of the annual Motor Show, together with the hill climbs, endurance runs, races and trials, drew considerable public attention in the newspapers and journals. The media were fascinated by the records set by racing car drivers at this time. It was Vauxhall's successes in racing in Russia in 1911 and 1912 which led to numerous sales in that country. Eventually an office was opened in Petrograd.

Today's ordering system is very fast, as can be seen by the following example. If a customer wants to buy an Astra he or she places the order with one of Vauxhall's retailers, detailing the model and any factory-fitted optional equipment. Vehicle orders can also be received from the Continent, as the plant is able to build left-hand drive Opel Astras for export.

Each order is processed by a mainframe computer in Europe, then relayed to Cheshire where it is stored in the Ellesmere Port plant's Data General Computer. Just 33 hours after the first piece of steel is pressed, the finished car leaves the line – fully inspected and tested. It then "passes into sales" and leaves the factory for direct delivery to the retailer in this country or to a port for export.

## Plowmans

A Vauxhall franchise in Luton was awarded to T. H. Plowman, Hitchin Road, in 1939. The garage owner, Thomas Plowman, had worked for Vauxhall as a tester. Thomas was out testing a Chrysler lorry chassis at Hockcliffe in 1922 when he came across a vehicle on fire and was badly burned rescuing the driver from the blazing wreck. He became a local hero and the donations which flooded in helped him to purchase his own garage in 1936.

He began to sell and race Vauxhall cars after the Second World War. The June 1948 edition of *The Vauxhall Motorist* pictures him driving his 24-year-old 30/98 Vauxhall at the Vintage Sports Club's Easter Monday speed trials at Luton Hoo where he scorched round the one-and-a-half mile twisting course in 91.5 seconds. The 30/98 had pride of place in his showrooms up to the late 1970s. Recently the car has been traced to Derbyshire, where it is in the showroom of a Bakewell garage.

In December 1992 Plowmans was taken over by partners Alan Sharp and Brian Arnold. They invested in a variety of new equipment including a £15,000 Sun diagnostic tuner for the workshop, a tyre fitting and balancing machine and an MOT bay offering a while-you-wait service to customers. In 1995 Plowmans changed hands again, this time its new owners were Caxton Motor Company.

At the Motor Show, Olympia, 1905, pictured above, 434 types of car were displayed at an average price of £600 with the most expensive costing £2,500. The Vauxhall stand can be seen in the foreground. Pictured below is the 1993 Motor Show at Earl's Court with the Vauxhall stand in the centre. At the 1905 show in November, Vauxhall introduced its first 4-cylinder car, an 18 hp motor costing £475, whilst at the 1993 Motor Show it displayed the Tigra concept car powered by a 1.6 litre ECOTEC engine and the Traka. The idea was to evaluate public response to these two new potential models and then decide whether to manufacture one or both vehicles.

1920s

1940s

1980s

1990s

*The evolution of the Vauxhall logo. The heraldic 1920s griffin was based on the crest of Fulk le Breant who was granted the manor of Luton by King John. Through marriage le Breant owned property in Lambeth on the south bank of the Thames where the Vauxhall Iron Works was later built. His Lambeth house and grounds were called Fulk's Hall, corrupted over the years to Fawke's Hall, later to Foxhall and ultimately Vauxhall. When in 1857 the Scottish engineer Alexander Wilson set up a business at the Vauxhall Iron Works in south London, he took the griffin as his company badge. The griffin badge returned to Luton when the company moved out of London in 1905!*

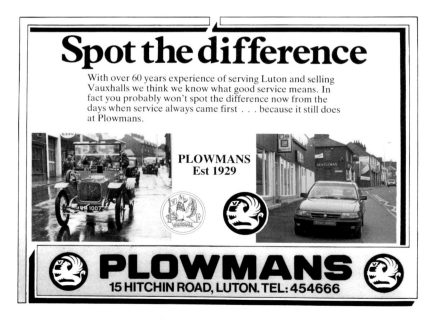

*Plowmans, Hitchin Road, Luton, advert, 1991. The petrol pumps had to be removed in the 1980s owing to fire regulations and the canopy was removed to make way for cars.*

On Saturday afternoon, June 6 1953, Lutonians thronged the streets from Manor Road to Wardown to watch the Coronation procession wind its way along. Nearly 70,000 people saw the Vauxhall Motors' carnival entry.

*A Vauxhall car being taken ashore in a surf boat, Accra, Ghana. Before the war the Hendon factory was used as Vauxhall's Export Boxing plant – the place where cars and trucks were packed for shipment overseas.*

*The frontage and showrooms of Shaw & Kilburn Limited, Cambridge Street, Aylesbury, late 1950s. The Cambridge Street site was purchased by Shaw & Kilburn from the existing Vauxhall dealer A. G. Bowker in 1945. The dealership has held the Vauxhall-Bedford franchises over the entire period. The full range of Bedford van and truck products were sold until the end of 1984 when truck sales were centralized at Shaw & Kilburn, Luton. In 1987 Shaw & Kilburn became part of the Lex Retail Group, following Lex's acquisition of the Sears Motor Group of which Shaw & Kilburn was part.*

# "AS VIRILE AS THEY COME"

JACK BRABHAM *Sunday Pictorial 20-5-62*

**"...I couldn't fault it. It is a good, sound, solid job that proved itself to me thoroughly in comfort, styling and roadholding.**

...Until very near maximum power output — a very beefy 113 brake horse power, incidentally — the engine hides away under the bonnet without a peep. Much of the smoothness, of course, comes from the six cylinders.

**...suddenly you wonder why you're all alone on the road. A quick glance at the speedo tells you— you're clocking over 80.**

*And 90-odd comes up before the rather shy 2.6 litre engine makes itself heard.*

## ...this car is as virile as they come"

**Two things you should know about the virile VELOX**

**1. The price:** £901.12.9 including tax. For that you get comfort for six, big-car power and safety to please even world champions—and, in Jack Brabham's hands, an average of 27 m.p.g.

**2. The way it handles.** This you can easily find out —give your Vauxhall dealer a ring and ask for a drive. Don't rush your trial; get to know the Velox. Enjoy the way it glides in traffic, then feel the push in the small of your back as it surges along the open road. The Velox is a big car. At a very reasonable price.

## VAUXHALL VELOX £901·12·9

And the more luxurious

## CRESTA £984·2·9

Friary Velox Estate Car £1,186.5.3
Friary Cresta Estate Car £1,270.16.6
EXTRAS
Hydra-matic* transmission £165.0.0
Laycock-de Normanville Overdrive £61.17.6
Power-assisted front disc brakes £20.12.6
*Prices include purchase tax.*
* *registered trademark*

*Advert in* Country Life, *July 19 1962.*

*Advert for the Vauxhall Victor, 1957. The* Bedfordshire Magazine *commented: "On the success of the Vauxhall Victor depend many Luton homes. It is the outcome of many months of design, planning and testing, as well as fantastic expenditure (some £16 million) in tooling the new factory at Luton. The long, low, sleek chassis introduces 'continental' design at a remarkably low basic price."*

*During the last few years Vauxhall advertising has been distinctive and memorable. Pictured here is an ad from Vauxhall's agency, Lowe Howard Spink.*

*Former Vauxhall employee Pete Worby, who acted as a double for Harrison Ford in the film* The Last Crusade, *delivers an Astra to the lucky winner of the BP Oil competition, 1990. Pete is in Indiana Jones costume, complete with whip, atop a giant raft on the lake at the National Exhibition Centre in Birmingham.*

### Sales

| Year | Total Output | Exports | Employees | Year | Total Output | Exports | Employees |
|------|------|------|------|------|------|------|------|
| 1903 | 43 | - | 150 | 1950 | 87,454 | 61,471 | 12,659 |
| 1906 | 15 | - | 180 | 1955 | 143,567 | 76,071 | 16,487 |
| 1907 | 69 | - | 200 | 1962 | 220,805 | 111,930 | 24,879 |
| 1920 | 689 | 97 | 1,023 | 1971 | 331,186 | 116,448 | 37,256 |
| 1925 | 1,388 | 95 | 1,820 | 1979 | 230,420 | 59,028 | 32,732 |
| 1935 | 48,671 | 15,314 | 6,726 | 1985 | 336,826 | 3,457 | 12,467 |
| | | | | 1994 | 427,441 | 93,494 | 9,917 |

# Sporting Successes

One of the earliest records in the Vauxhall archives is a certificate given by Wolverhampton and District AC that "Mr A. E. Price successfully drove a 5 hp Vauxhall car No. 4 weighing 701 lbs with two passengers weighing 330 lbs up the above (Hermitage Hill) in five minutes 46 seconds, on Saturday the 24th day of October, 1903".

In 1904, Vauxhall director Percy Kidner tested the new 6 hp model in the Glasgow to London run. The Vauxhall was the smallest car entered and during the whole trial only seven marks out of 1,000 were lost (one mark was deducted for each minute taken to change a plug). *Autocar* gave special mention to the Vauxhall for its overall performance in the trial. Petrol consumption was 38.25 mpg.

Hill climbs, endurance runs, races and trials figured prominently in those early years. They drew considerable attention as the public were excited by the novelty of record breaking. In February 1908, details of the 2,000 miles RAC Trials were published and Vauxhall decided to design and enter a new car for this event.

This trial, which lasted 15 days, started in London and linked up with the Scottish Reliability Trials in Glasgow. There were some timed hill climbs in Scotland and the Lake District and finally a speed test of some 200 miles round Brooklands. Vauxhall entered one car, which was originally described as a 12/16 hp. However, a 20 hp car was run. This was the brainchild of engineering genius, Laurence Pomeroy. The Vauxhall lost fewer marks in this event than any other car. Throughout the entire trial the car "did not have one involuntary stop for any mechanical reason including replenishment of oil and water". Marks were only lost for refilling with petrol. It became the most discussed car of the year.

During the next six years Laurence Pomeroy produced two outstanding vehicles based on the development of the 20 hp car. They were the "C" type which became known as The Prince Henry and the 30/98.

The Vauxhall team led by Percy Kidner won many trials, hill climbs and track events during the period 1909–1914. Members of this team included A. J. Hancock, W. Watson, F. W. Hodges and R. Seltz. Success in Russia in 1911 and 1912 led to numerous sales there and the eventual opening of an office in Petrograd.

The 30/98 notched up an impressive string of motor sport successes in the early 1920s. Between 1920 and 1923 it scored over 70 outright wins and 52 seconds in major hill climbs and speed trials. In 1924 Vauxhall withdrew from motor sport, at the height of the 30/98's success. This was due to the high cost of motor racing together with a shrinking market for high priced, high performance cars.

Saloon car champion, Bill Blydenstein, not only drove cars but also prepared the cars. He started Vauxhall's racing revival with the VX4/90 and in 1965 with the HA Viva. Development of the HB in 1967 for Vauxhall dealers, Shaw & Kilburn, followed. Blydenstein began to concentrate on preparing cars while Gerry Marshall raced them. At the end of 1969 Marshall was runner-up in the Saloon Car Championship. In 1971 Vivas won all the major saloon car championships.

Dealer Team Vauxhall was formed in 1971 to race Vauxhall saloons. In 1973 they added rallies to their original saloon car races. In 1979 Pentti Airikkala won the British Open Rally Championship, in a Chevette. The competition consisted of seven international rallies in the UK and Ireland.

Vauxhall continues to pursue an active programme of sports sponsorship. In 1994 the Vauxhall Sport rally driver team of David Llewellyn and Ian Grindrod in the Vauxhall Astra GSi won three titles in the Formula 2 category of the Mobil/Top Gear British Rally Championship. After tough rounds in Wales, Scotland, Ireland and Isle of Man, they won the F2 Drivers', F2 Co-drivers' and the Manufacturers' titles.

## LONDON TO BRIGHTON RUN

The London to Brighton Vintage car run is held every year to celebrate the "emancipation" of the motor car. Prior to this date a man holding a red flag had to walk 100 yards in front of the car to warn people of the horseless carriage's approach.

In November 1896 the law changed and the need for a man walking in front of the car was abolished and the speed limit raised to 12 mph. To celebrate this freedom of the road the newly-formed Motor Car Club organized a run from London to Brighton on the day the new law came into force, Saturday, November 14. The race is still run

every year and is known as the RAC Veteran Car Run. About 460 cars take part each year. Vauxhall's 1904 car, which runs every year, only just qualifies as no car made after December 31 1904 can enter.

In 1992 Vauxhall Motors' senior vehicle restorer, Bernard Ridgley, talked to the *Luton News* about the run. Bernard, who coaxes the best out of the 1904 Vauxhall, which is the oldest motor at Vauxhall, said:

"I get up a good old speed, 15 mph! The modern cars pull in front of you so that the children in the back can have a good look. That is when I am terrified of their red lights coming on. Modern cars have something new, like brakes on front wheels. That is terrible. They can stop on a sixpence. In my old girl I need the length of a cricket pitch to stop and I am frightened of rolling into the back of them.

"It looks fun but it is not easy driving a motor with no steering wheel, no brakes worth speaking of, two gears and no fan to cool the engine. There are some steep hills and that is another problem. Redhill is a real terror but fortunately there is a Vauxhall dealership there so I always stop and have a cup of coffee and give the little girl time to cool off."

*Vauxhall Heritage's oldest car, a two-gear tiller-steered car built in 1904, at the start of the London to Brighton Veteran Car Run, 1994. The car has taken part in the race regularly since 1950, and has only once failed to make the run in the time allowed, and that was due to a broken axle.*

*P. C. Kidner and A. J. Hancock, pictured in 1908 at Brooklands at the completion of the RAC and Scottish Reliability Trials. This Vauxhall was the first car in the world, of any make, to complete 2,000 miles without an involuntary stop.*

*By the end of 1909 Vauxhall produced a streamlined single-seater body. The car was fitted with a 3-litre engine and A. J. Hancock, pictured above, managed a flying half-mile at 88.62 mph. The car was nicknamed "KN".*

*In October 1910 A. J. Hancock in a similar car, with output boosted to 60 bhp, managed 100 mph at Brooklands. It was the first 20 hp car of any make in the world to exceed 100 mph. Note the wheel discs which were an asset in conditions when brake cooling was not yet at a premium.*

*Boyd Edkins sits behind the wheel of his 16/20 hp Vauxhall in which he broke the Melbourne-Sydney record by two hours seven minutes at an average speed of 34 mph for the 570 miles.*

*A. J. Hancock at the driving wheel of the 3.3-litre GP Vauxhall during the 1914 Isle of Man TT race.*

*In 1922 this Vauxhall took part in the Isle of Man TT races. At the wheel is E. Swain, Assistant Chief Inspector.*

This silver salver has inscribed on it all the victories won by the Vauxhall team between 1909 and 1925. It is interesting to note that the salver was made by melting down most of the trophies awarded to the firm's drivers during those years.

A 1904 Vauxhall completes the hill climb run by the Sporting Owner Drivers' Club in Woburn Park, 1968.

*Manx Trophy Rally, 1977. Finnish team leader Pentti Airikkala wins for Dealer Team Vauxhall in a Blydenstein-tuned 2300HS Chevette. Risto Virtanen is in the passenger seat.*

*Tina Thorner and Louise Aitken-Walker celebrate victory in the 1990 RAC Rally. Louise Aitken-Walker was the first woman home, finishing 17th overall and clinching the FIA Ladies World Cup. She won the two-litre class by a massive 35 minutes in her Astra 16v.*

*Formula Vauxhall Lotus action at Donington Park, 1990. For the 1991 season Vauxhall Motors and Mobil provided a prize fund and support package worth over £12,000 for the 15-race championship of the Vauxhall 2-litre, 16-valve cars.*

*The late Dave Metcalfe takes the Nova to 14th spot in the tough 1,400 mile four-day event RAC Rally in 1990.*

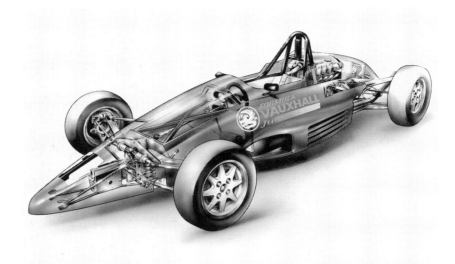

*Vauxhall's formula junior car. This took to the tracks for the first time in 1991 with a support package and prize fund of over £40,000. The 1600 cc Nova GSi-engined single seaters were a favourite choice for those seeking a first step on the motor racing ladder of success.*

*1993 Corsa Rally Cross car pictured at the Motor Show. For the technically minded it has a Corsa 3-door bodyshell, 1600 cc single cam engine developing 160 bhp at 7,000 rpm. The car is fitted with a corbeam seat, 5-speed gearbox and Avon rallycross control tyres with a strengthened roll cage. It has MacPherson struts with de Carbon dampers, uses Mobil 1 oil and Mobil unleaded fuel and weighs 700 kg.*

*Vauxhall display at the 1993 Motor Show with Vauxhall sport karting (foreground) for 8-12 year olds. Speeds of 50 mph can be obtained. In the background is the Dallara 393 Formula 3 racing car with a Vauxhall 2-litre, 16 valve twin overhead cam.*

# Industrial Relations

## Pre-1920

A strike by 427 women workers at the Chaul End Munitions factory owned by Vauxhall took place on Friday, May 26 1916 and Monday, May 29 1916. The firm, which was under Government control, locked out the workers when 427 out of the 467 women did not return after the Friday midday meal. The women remained in the works yard, singing, booing and demonstrating – without lodging any complaint. The strike stemmed from poor working conditions and low pay, the highest rate being about 18s 10d for a 54-hour week. One of the foremen had previously been told that the women would come out on strike unless they were given a halfpenny an hour rise.

The women went back to work on the Tuesday but 17 of them, namely: Maggie Gore, Olive Cannon, E. Browne, Blanche Stimpson, May Ellingham, Ursula Blackburn, Florence Isaacs, Grace Breading, Grace Thompson, Ethel Greatholder, Lily Chapman, Cissie Blake, Lily Pakes, Gladys Warren, E. Tansley, Adelene Thompson and Violet Lawrence, found themselves before a Westminster tribunal the following week accused of being absent from work. This contravened Government regulations about war work.

The tribunal judge, while recognizing that the women's strike was illegal, strongly criticized the management, especially Edward H. Bolton, manager of the department, and only fined the girls one shilling instead of a possible £5 a day he was capable of imposing.

## 1920-1950

The following notes are largely based on the research undertaken by Len Holden:

Between 1920 and 1950 there were no industrial disputes of any significance but Len's research suggests that Vauxhall was not the ideal employer. Len asked Vauxhall for the Board Room Meeting Minutes and other "sensitive" information concerning industrial relations. He was "politely but firmly told that this information was highly confidential and these records were entombed in a nuclear bomb-proof shelter somewhere within a 20-mile radius of Luton".

In the 1920s Vauxhall employees found that if they held a trade union card, and management found out, then they were instantly dismissed. Harold Horne recalled that stories were told of how, at any time of the day, they'd come to the end of a run because of a shortage of material or whatever. The foreman would then come round with a board saying 3 o'clock which meant that everybody clocked out and went home at that time.

During the 1926 General Strike, people who had trade union membership came out on strike. Many of them were dismissed after the General Strike was over. Workers were still discomforted in 1929. One ex-employee recalled that it was hell in those days as men could be sacked for washing their hands as the hooter blew.

During the 1930s many British industries in the North, Scotland and South Wales were in deep depression. Many unemployed young workers travelled to growth areas such as Luton in search of a job. Swansea-born, Glyn Morgan, recalled:

"There was a massive influx of people from unemployed areas, and recruitment at Vauxhall from about 1934 until the outbreak of the war was about 75 per cent to 80 per cent immigrant. The Scottish accent was commonplace. Scottish societies and

Presbyterian churches sprang up in Luton. It must have been one of the quickest-growing areas in Britain. One man I knew, Jimmy Cooper, he walked every inch of the way from Glasgow, on his own to get a job."

Vauxhall was paying good wages – up to £3 a week compared with £1 18s at Kent Instruments. It is not surprising that in the 1930s and 1940s people were clamouring to get jobs at Vauxhall. There was always a queue outside the Employment Office.

Charles Bartlett, a British appointment by General Motors, was Managing Director from 1930 until 1953. He had at his command a relatively docile labour force who were paid relatively good wages in a town without strong trade union traditions.

The Group Bonus System was introduced by him in the 1930s. The workers worked in groups and each man's wage was calculated on the basis of the production of the group as a whole. All the operations were studied twice and if the men were over 100 per cent efficient they were entitled to a 25 per cent bonus. However, if they were below target they lost one-and-a-half per cent of the bonus. This system helped produce more of a team effort. Peter Vigor, who spent some time as a capstan operator, recalls:

"If somebody talked or distracted another worker, the others in the group would shout 'cuckoo, cuckoo' because they thought he was fouling the nest. Also lateness was disapproved of by banging the chuck key so that all the group knew you were late."

Charles Bartlett's right-hand man, Reginald Pearson (later, Sir Reginald), who was promoted from off the shop floor, said of him:

"I considered him a great man. He was a man's man. He was easy to talk to – both management and men. He knew many of the men by their Christian names – how many kids they had, if their kids were ill, and so on."

In 1941 Bartlett set up the Management Advisory Committee. This was a committee of representatives from the shop floor who met regularly with management to discuss grievances and problems of the work-force. It was effective in smoothing relations between management and men but it was phased out in the early 1960s.

Bartlett also introduced a Profit Sharing Scheme, which began in 1935. The idea was to share a portion of the profits among the work-force at the end of each year in the form of a Christmas bonus. This was done to encourage employees to feel greater loyalty to the company. Peter Vigor remembers:

"It was the most eagerly awaited notice of the whole year. My brother bought a bicycle under this scheme."

However, for a number of years no bonuses were paid at all. In the 1950s it was replaced by another agreement.

The main unions at Vauxhall were the Amalgamated Engineering Union (later the AEUW) and the National Union of Vehicle Builders (NUVB). As union membership increased the problem of "poaching" members led to designation of recruitment areas. The NUVB tended to have the body shops and the AEU had the machine shops.

At the end of the Second World War the first big dispute occurred. Harold Horne recalled:

"The first big strike, in which I played a fairly major role incidentally, was in, I think, 1945. It started in the body shop over the bonus prices for finished vehicles. This strike was really a turning point, as far as labour relations were concerned. It was never the same after this. Bartlett, with a certain amount of arrogance believed he could solve this, and he came down to a meeting in the body shop at which I was speaking. At the time I was chairman of the Vauxhall Shop Stewards Committee. We allowed him to get up on the box to talk to the workers, and he believed that just by talking to them he could get them to go back to work, but he got a bit of a shock and somebody called out from the back of the meeting 'We don't want management here. This is a workers' meeting.' And he had to retreat. A big meeting was held in the canteen after the strike had been on a few days. A settlement was arrived at whereby payments of bonus were improved."

## 1970–1995

During the 1970s Vauxhall continued to be bedevilled by industrial relations problems. Regular strikes of suppliers occurred and at the plant itself. The strength of the unions was demonstrated in 1976 when a Vauxhall security guard who was good at his job of spotting petty pilfering had to be moved to another job after strike threats at the factory. Towards the end of 1979 Vauxhall hit an all-time low with a three-month strike, reaching the company's "make or break" point. Fortunately, determined action by management and a realistic response from the work-force helped put the company back on its feet. This was helped by a constantly improving product range and a constant upturn in the UK economy.

Charlie Golden, the then present Chairman and Managing Director of Vauxhall, recalled in a recent interview printed in the *Luton News* Vauxhall Souvenir Supplement:

"I had a relationship with Vauxhall long before I came here, when I was dealing with international operations. It was one of the parts of GM where we had a little trouble . . .

"Labour relations were poor. Some of the products were not so good. The fact that Vauxhall had designed and engineered products that had been good for a long time could not compensate when competition started to increase dramatically, particularly from the Japanese.

"As a unit Vauxhall was too small and had to become European instead of English. We

had to pool design expertise and get into bigger volume production.

"It forced great changes to be made but GM knew it had to turn Vauxhall round by identifying the problems and coming up with solutions. The cashflow was, you might say, very negative!

"Vauxhall was one of the bigger problems we had then, but now it is just the opposite – it is one of the best companies in the whole of General Motors.

"We owe others, including the work-force at the time, a great debt. The turn-a-round started in the early 1980s when basic agreements were reached between management and unions to change working practices.

"The product became better and better, marketing improved and the profits started to come.

"By the early 1990s a lot of progress had been made, with the team-working agreement adding to it in 1992.

"Vauxhall was very profitable because it had a high-quality product which did well in this country and was exported all over Europe as well. Investment was made to modernize Vauxhall. We got rid of the old tired-looking buildings to produce an up-to-date facility. The work-force and management changed; every one knows what it takes to succeed, and be profitable. We have good stable relationships."

The management of today is much more aware of the need to communicate with people. The company negotiates with three trade unions, the TGWU, the MSF and the AEEU. Meetings are held every two months at national level, and monthly in individual plants. The annual round of negotiations has now been replaced by two-year deals. Today Vauxhall workers are top of the league in pay, with Jaguar being the only other company near the company's rates.

In December 1995 Vauxhall workers rejected a pay offer which led to an overtime ban and the loss of 1,700 vehicles with a showroom value of £22 million. About half of these were lost at the Luton factory.

*Vauxhall girls on strike for higher pay in 1916. The notes on the back of the photograph state that "the strike resulted in their wages of £1 per week being raised, after the strikers were taken to court and fined 1s. Mrs Dorothy Clarke was the instigator and leader. She came to Luton in 1914. Life in domestic service did not appeal to her. She was unable to do straw plait so she took a job at Vauxhall and joined the trade union."*

*In November 1970 over 1,000 protestors marched under a railway bridge advertising the company with whom they are in dispute. The sacking of 325 white-collar workers caused DATA union members to march to the Kimpton Road factory. Today DATA no longer exists, but in those days it was the campaigning white-collar union.*

*In March 1963 hundreds of skilled workers, mainly from "X" block which included the die shop, the jig shop, experimental and styling, walked out of the factory gates to attend an unofficial protest meeting in the Park Street sports ground (below). They were protesting about the $3^1/_2 d$ an hour increase awarded to them by management. They were also unhappy about there being no offer of a 40-hour week or of a three-week holiday for all skilled workers.*

*Monday, January 4 1965 saw some 12,000 of the 21,000 workers meet on Pope's Meadow. They had been locked out after saying they would walk out. The dispute over pay resulted int he assembly lines being idle for the first time since the 1926 General Strike. The workers returned to work the following day. The one-day stoppage cost Vauxhall about 1,500 vehicles and a loss in money terms of approximately £750,000.*

*DATA, the Draughtsmen's and Allied Trades Association white-collar union, organize a big demonstration by Vauxhall draughtsmen protesting against redundancies, March 1967. The anti-American banner sums up the feeling of the men. At the mass meeting on the Osborne Road car park members expressed fears that design work on future Vauxhall models would be transferred to Opel, the General Motors' subsidiary.*

# Ellesmere Port

In 1959 when average weekly earnings for hourly-paid Vauxhall employees were £17 15s 3d and the company was expanding rapidly, the Government prohibited expansion in south Bedfordshire. The Board of Trade decided to use Vauxhall's future growth as a means to further Government policy of bringing work to depressed or designated areas i.e. an area where there are more workers than jobs. The company was given little choice and settled on Ellesmere Port near Liverpool with the view to transferring there the commercial vehicle side of production. The main centre, however, was still to remain in south Bedfordshire.

By the autumn of 1961 a change of policy had been announced by Vauxhall Motors. It now intended to keep its Bedford truck and van production at the Dunstable works. The Cheshire factory would now act as a "feeder" for the Luton and Dunstable plants, producing mechanical components for both cars and trucks.

Work began that same year on the complete new car plant at Ellesmere Port on Merseyside. The Ellesmere Port plant was built on the site of the wartime airfield at Hooton near the Manchester Ship Canal and River Mersey. Production of components began there in 1963, car assembly a year later with the first Viva being produced on June 1 1964.

The HA Viva was the first evidence of the growing collaboration between Vauxhall and its sister GM company, Adam Opel in Germany. The Viva engine design was taken from the unit used in the Opel Kadett. The last Viva was produced in 1979.

Today the 400-acre plant employs around 4,500 people and has become the only General Motors facility in Europe to produce the entire range of new Astra cars and vans.

The Astra range is pressed, assembled, painted and trimmed at the Ellesmere Port plant beginning with the arrival of high quality steel by road. The panels which form the body of the vehicle are produced on a massive 1,600 tonne Tri-Axis Transfer Press and High-speed Coil Cut Line. In the paint shop the body shell moves through a series of timed, pre-arranged processes. After the paint shop, badges and decals are applied by hand. Next, in trim, the vehicle has the cockpit and door modules added before final assembly completes the construction with the addition of the remaining mechanical units. The car is extensively checked before it receives its seal of approval.

In 1994 the plant expanded its manufacturing base, accelerating output of the ECOTEC V6 engine, engine components, sheet metal sub-assemblies and axles. About 90 per cent of the plant's component output goes to export markets. The plant also celebrated the production of its two-and-a-half millionth vehicle in 1994 – just 30 years after the first car left Ellesmere Port.

*Tom Behan, boiler operator, checks the dials of boiler No. 1 at Ellesmere Port, 1967.*

*Another milestone in 1981 was the start of Astra production at Ellesmere Port, earlier Astras having been imported from Opel. The Cheshire plant was now building both Chevette and Astra ranges.*

*Prime Minister John Major presents on behalf of management a silver salver to Works Manager, Mike Chapman, marking Ellesmere Port's record output in 1990, which he received on behalf of all the work-force. Picture taken February 1991.*

*In February 1990 the new buzz-word at Ellesmere Port plant was continuous improvement. The engine trim area was the first to give the revolutionary new work process a try.*

*New press shop, Ellesmere Port, about 1991. Using state-of-the-art technology, and weighing 1,600 tonnes, this Large Transfer Press carries out the work of four conventional press lines and produces up to 16 body panels per minute. It takes just 33 hours after the first piece of steel is pressed for the finished car to leave the line, fully inspected and tested.*

*New paint shop, Ellesmere Port, about 1991. Verification operators closely examine the paintwork on the Astra to ensure that the high quality controls and degree of mirrored finish from the advanced paint formulations are maintained at all times.*

# Unusual Vehicles

In February 1991 the Vauxhall *Mirror* published the following article about the one remaining Vauxhall motorbike:

❝One man's obsession has saved the only Vauxhall motorbike in existence.

Bob Thomas remembers his uncle, who used to work for Vauxhall, talking about a special motorbike. That was in the mid-1920s when he was a toddler.

Nearly 20 years later, Bob tracked down one of only two complete machines built at Luton in 1921.

The bike was produced when Vauxhall gave designers Ricardo the task of designing a super car and a super motorbike.

The result was a sleek 950 cc, four cylinder, overhead valve machine which the company decided was too expensive to ever go into production.

When Bob discovered it, the bike was not in the peak of condition – in fact, it was in bits!

One of the previous owners was a London chauffeur.

"He used to take the motorbike apart every year for overhaul," said Bob. One year while he was doing this, he died!

"The man who bought the bits left them outside his house, allowing wartime salvage hunters to make away with the frame. All I got was the engine, gearbox and wheels."

Bob asked Vauxhall for the original plans and designs and set about reconstructing the machine.

Engineers at Vauxhall helped by making a petrol tank and by 1957, the only Vauxhall motorbike still in existence was part of Bob's collection in the home of motorcycle racing, the Isle of Man.

"It's the pride of the pack," he said. "A beautiful machine that was far ahead of its time. In fact modern motorbikes are coming back to this sort of design."

The bike has been widely exhibited, and Bob still rides it in vintage and club rallies.

And what of the other Vauxhall motorbike? Unfortunately, it was destroyed by a firm of breakers in 1935. "They just didn't value it in those days," said Bob.❞

*Stan Brown and the Vauxhall workers fit a new petrol tank in 1957.*

*Earl of Ranfurly suggested this idea for a motor hansom. Vauxhall built this model in 1905 and showed it at Olympia that November.* Autocar *rated the design "well adapted to the use of medical practitioners". A London cab company did order five but by summer 1906 they had been discarded, no doubt due to their long and woolly linkages. The prototype pictured here ended its days collecting the factory wages from Lloyds Bank in Luton. The wages were taken to a vault in Kimpton Road where they were guarded night and day. The money was paid out every Friday to Vauxhall workers. Today salaries are paid electronically through banks and no cash is paid out.*

*Another adaptation of the hansom-cab, this time with the driver sitting over the engine and the fuel tank set high up at the rear. Note that solid tyres are used at the back. This layout leaves no room for flutes, which were inspired by the motif on a director's wardrobe, about 1905.*

*The Morgan "Flitwick" sports two-seater, about 1919. This sports body, built entirely to customers' instructions, was fitted on to a Vauxhall 30/98 chassis by the Leighton Buzzard company, Morgan & Co.*

*Another Vauxhall chassis which is almost certainly an Imperial model with bodywork by Mulliner of London. The 20 hp chassis is from the 1910/11 period.*

*This picture shows John Bassett (right), owner of Chiltern Cars, Leighton Buzzard, and T. Skevington, with a 1923 vintage Vauxhall 30/98 they had spent months renovating in 1968. The car, which was capable of 90 mph, was auctioned for £3,000.*

*A disabled person tries out the Astra Assessment Module.*

# Bouquet Letters

The BBC's best-known war correspondent, Martin Bell, wrote to Vauxhall in 1992 praising the Carlton he used to cover the war in what used to be Yugoslavia. He wrote:

"Despite the attentions of the local drivers, who smashed in the nearside doors, and snipers, who riddled it with bullet and mortar fragment holes, the car ran like a champ, took us everywhere in impossible circumstances and out–performed the UN's armoured personnel carriers on the mountain roads beyond no-man's land.

"We have since had to replace the Carlton with an armoured vehicle of our own. But I did not want it to pass into history without a big thank you to Vauxhall."

Vauxhall pensioner, David Norris, a former Dealer Development Manager, recalled recently to a *Luton News* reporter his fond memories about his 1935 DX Light Six, which he bought for just £35 in 1957:

"It was a great little car. The reliability sticks in my memory and I recall my wife, Isabel, and I once travelling all the way to Hartlepool in it.

"I kept the Light Six for a few months – eventually receiving the first Victor model as a company car – and sold the 1935 car to my brother-in-law for £12 and a washing machine!"

In January 1991 Mr H. Thatcher of Rossendale, Lancs, wrote a letter of praise to the Vauxhall *Mirror* about his 1982 Chevette:

"I would like to let you know how well satisfied I am with Vauxhall cars I have had up to the present: never had a better model.

"My present model is a 1982 Chevette which I bought as a demonstrator model and have had for eight years.

"I have done 500 miles over 100,000 and it has never let me down.

"The engine has not had any repairs to it. The clutch is still the original. There are not many motors to compare with that. Even the paintwork is the original, and still good.

"To anyone wishing to buy a new car, I can recommend the Vauxhalls for their excellent reliability.

"I hope you will appreciate the performance of a car made by Vauxhall Motors, which still remains a proud possession of my family."

In March 1993 the *Luton News* reported that Vauxhall Motors was publicly thanked by a Luton mother at the centre of a sensational "car-jacking" case. The victim's car was set on fire by two youths after they sexually assaulted and robbed her during a three-hour terror drive. Her white Astra was destroyed so she contacted Vauxhall about hiring a vehicle. Vauxhall Consumer Affairs Consultant, Jean Gouldthorpe, arranged for the loan, free of charge, of a brand new Vauxhall Nova. The Luton mother told the reporter:

"I couldn't afford to be without a car and Vauxhall bent over backwards to help me. They weren't after publicity, but so many firms are slagged-off these days I thought it would be nice to praise a local company who offered to help someone in need. They even delivered the car and picked it up when I had finished with it."

In June 1991 the Vauxhall *Mirror* published the following letter and photograph from a delighted Dr D. T. Vethanayagam, of Tamilnadu, India:

"Please find a snap-shot of my Vauxhall Velox car purchased in August 1949 which is in continuous use by me and my family. Standing beside this immaculate car are my wife and I. On the bonnet of the car is a valuable sports cup won by this car at an exhibition of vintage and classic cars organised by the Government Tourism Department and the 'Vintage Classic Vehicles Foundation of India' at the 17th India Tourist and Industrial Fair at The Island Grounds, Madras, after a rally cum exhibition in January.

"There were several vintage cars participating in the rally and drive along the Mount Road and Marina Beach Road, finally ending up at the Island Grounds Fair for exhibition. This car was at the vanguard of the procession of cars.

"It is to be noted that this was the only car to keep moving silently along the non-stop run, whereas, other cars had to stop, with their radiator water boiling and some needing pushing to get their engines started!

"I purchased this car at Messrs Sundaram Motors Ltd, Madras, in August 1949. It was one of six such cars to be imported from England, and my car was the first to be sold by the firm.

"The engine is smooth and was rebored only once in its life."

# Bedford Vehicles

The first commercial vehicle to have the Bedford name appeared in April 1931 from the Luton factory. The first model was a 2-tonner with a choice of two wheelbases - the WHG at 131 ins and WLG at 157 ins. The Bedford name was almost certainly derived from the county in which Vauxhall Motors had operated since 1905.

Sales of Bedford trucks provided most of the company's profits before the introduction of the Light Six in 1933 and Vauxhall Ten in 1937. It is interesting to note that British-built Chevrolet trucks had been produced at Luton since 1929. However, when Bill Knudsen, the President of Chevrolet, was visiting England in 1930, he reacted angrily when he discovered that Chevrolet truck production had gone ahead without his permission. He immediately ordered Vauxhall to cease manufacturing Chevrolet components. By the end of 1931 Bedford had ousted the 12 cwt and 30 cwt Chevrolets from the assembly lines in Luton.

In August 1931 modified versions of the two truck chassis in the form of 14 and 20-seater bodies (WHB and WLB) were launched. They were very successful and 52 per cent of all 14/20 seater buses and coaches registered in the last quarter were Bedfords. In April 1932 the 30 cwt WS chassis and 12 cwt Light Delivery van were launched. In 1932 Bedfords were being exported to Japan, China, Borneo, Iceland and Russia as well as many European and Commonwealth countries.

In June 1933 an 8 cwt van was available. This van was developed from the 12 and 14 hp Vauxhall Light Six cars. The following November saw the launch of new 3-ton models at the Commercial Vehicle Show in London. These new models set the pattern for British medium-sized commercial vehicles and took Bedford into the early 1950s with few major changes.

In 1966 the KM range took Bedford into the 22/24 ton class. The two-millionth Bedford was produced in 1969. Bedford went on to enter the premium heavy truck business with the TM models and reached its three-millionth vehicle in 1978.

In 1983 a new Bedford Commercial Vehicle Division, separate from Vauxhall Motors Limited, was created as a Commercial Vehicle Corporation. This operated as a separate GM company in the UK.

The new van plant at Luton was formally opened on January 23 1985. The Midi and CF2 vans were produced here. Production began in February 1986 of the little Rascal van.

In order to survive the depressed markets GM and Bedford management realized that a partner would be needed to provide Bedford with the volume base necessary to provide a viable future.

IBC Vehicles was formed in 1987 as a joint venture between General Motors and Isuzu Motors of Japan. Since then the new company has invested in excess of £100 million in new facilities and product improvement.

The van factory at Kimpton Road produces the Vauxhall Midi medium van and passenger wagon range, the Vauxhall Rascal as well as the Frontera and Frontera Sport. The major reason for the company's success is the Frontera four-wheel drive leisure vehicle. The introduction of the Frontera in 1991 has led to the work-force increasing from 1,750 to 2,400 in July 1993. Luton IBC celebrated selling its 200,000th vehicle on June 9 1993.

IBC sells its vehicles to Opel and Vauxhall which distribute them throughout Europe. In fact, 80 per cent of production is for export to Continental markets, with Germany being the most important market.

The truck plant at Dunstable was taken over by David J. B. Brown as a going concern in 1987 and renamed AWD Limited. The new company concentrated on civilian truck production. Unfortunately five years later in 1992 the company was wound-up with the loss of over 500 jobs. The Bedford name, however, has survived and is used on trucks produced by Marshall SPV, Cambridge.

## Landmarks in Bedford Story

1931 Enter the first Bedfords: 2-ton trucks (WHG and WLG) and two bus chassis (WHB and WLB).

1932 30 cwt truck (WS) and 12 cwt vans (VY/VX) added to range. Bedfords accounted for half of all British commercial vehicle exports.

1933 3-ton trucks (WT), and 8 cwt vans (ASY, ASX) introduced.

1935 26-seater bus chassis (WTB) joins range.

1938 5/6 cwt van (HC) introduced.

1939 New 10/12 cwt van (JC) introduced. OB coach (briefly).

1939-45 Over 250,000 Bedford trucks built for Forces, plus 5,640 Churchill tanks.

1946 K, M and O models in production. Range now includes 5-ton trucks and tractor unit for articulated vehicles. OB 26-seater coach chassis.

1947 500,000th Bedford truck produced. First British manu-facturer to reach that number.

1950 "Big Bedford" S-type 7-ton truck models and 10-ton tractor unit introduced – Bedford's first forward-control civilian models. 32/40-seater bus chassis (SB) added to range.

1952 10 cwt CA van introduced; first non-car derived light van from any British manu-facturer. First 4 x 4 civilian truck introduced (the R-type).

1953 New A-type Middleweights replace K, M and O range.

1955 Production facilities greatly increased by transfer of truck production from Luton to Dunstable. 64,773 Bedfords produced;

more in one year than any other British make.

1957 Two entirely new 6-ton truck models introduced (D and C models). Normal and forward control. First Bedford-built diesel engines introduced, the 300 cu in and 200 cu in units.

1958 1,000,000th Bedford comes off the line. TJ normal-control models introduced.

1960 TK trucks and tractor units introduced. Output of Bedfords exceeded 100,000 units a year for the first time.

1961 New VAS 30-seater coach chassis introduced.

1962 VAL twin-steer coach chassis introduced for 52/55 seaters.

1964 6 cwt and 8 cwt HA vans introduced.

1965 VAM 45-seat coach chassis introduced.

1966 KM range of heavy trucks takes Bedford into the 22/24-ton class.

1968 KM 6 x 2 introduced.

1969 2,000,000th Bedford produced – of which 1,500,000 were trucks. CF van range introduced.

1970 M-type 4 x 4 truck and first underfloor engine coach chassis introduced (YRQ).

1971 KM range expanded by introduction of 6 x 4 models.

1974 Introduction of first phase of TM range of premium trucks and tractor units (Detroit Diesel 6V-71 models).

1975 Phase 2 TMs introduced (500 engine models). Bedford's 500 engine for TK, KM and coach chassis. 140 in wheelbase model added to CF range.

1976 Phase 3 TMs introduced (Detroit Diesel 8V-71 models). JJL Midi Bus announced. Van range widened by introduction of Chevanne. GM diesel engine introduced for CF range.

1978 The year of the three millionth. 1,000,000th Bedford van built. 2,000,000th Bedford truck built – of which over 500,000 were TKs. Record total for a British truck make and record total for British truck model.

1980 New TL range of medium-weight trucks, 5 to 16.3 tonnes. £8,000,000 expansion programme started at Dunstable.

1981 Golden Jubilee Rally held at Luton to mark 50 years of Bedford production.

1982 The TM "heavies" were enlarged. The 1,500,000th Bedford was exported.

1983 Bedford no longer part of Vauxhall Motors. A new Bedford Commercial Vehicle Division was created, part of General Motors. £70,000,000 million improvement plan announced.

1984 The CF2 medium van, a new car-derived Astra van and all-new 1-tonne Midi van shown at 1984 UK Motor Show.

1985 Inauguration of new van plant at Luton.

1987 IBC Vehicles formed as a joint venture between GM and Isuzu to run the van plant. Truck plant at Dunstable sold to David Brown as a going concern and renamed AWD Limited.

*The first WS 30 cwt Bedford being christened before leaving the works in April 1932. The 30 cwt chassis sold for £175 and a dropside truck for £210.*

*The first 5/6 cwt HC Bedford about to be driven away from the works, 1938. The van gave over 35 mpg fully laden and offered 70 cu ft of load space. Costing £140 this was the first 4-cylinder Bedford and the first to have independent front suspension.*

*1935: Assembling Bedford engines at the Luton factory where Vauxhall cars and Bedford trucks were designed and made.*

*One of the first Bedford two-tonners at work in 1931. This one is the shorter version – 131 in wheelbase (WHG). For five months this particular truck carried pipes for a Rhondda Valley sewage scheme along the bed of the River Taff.*

*1936 Bedford 12-15 cwt van, 22 hp owned by J. Ovel from Soursham, Huntingdon, pictured at Woburn Abbey in 1991.*

*The original flat-nosed Bedford undergoing Army trials shortly before the start of the Second World War. The vehicle allowed certain non-standard truck items to be housed under the bonnet.*

*1941 Bedford 4 x 4 QL military GS C owned by R. Woodcock, Ampthill, pictured at Woburn Abbey in 1991.*

*Rt Hon G. R. Strauss, MP, Minister of Supply, drives the 500,000th Bedford off the assembly line at Luton, Wednesday, October 22 1947. In his speech to the workers he emphasized that every car exported meant a week's meat ration for 10,000 fellow citizens. Also in the cab of the Bedford was the Vauxhall employee, Arthur Fountain, who had driven off the very first Bedford truck ever built, back in April 1931.*

*A "Siamese twin" 3-ton Bedford chassis in service in China, 1946. The vehicle ran on train wheels and was adapted for use on the Kowloon-Canton railway between Taipo and Fanling.*

*An old and new Bedford. On the left is a 5/6 cwt HC Bedford van run by R. Jellis and Son, Family Butchers (established 1931), Old Farm, Pitstone. The HC was produced from 1938 to 1948. On its right is the Bedford Rascal panel van introduced in the 1980s.*

These two vehicles are S-type "Big Bedfords" first seen at the 1950 Commercial Motor Show. These 4-wheelers were capable of carrying a full seven tons and still within the 30 mph category. The rather high bulbous one-piece cab was to remain a familiar sight on our roads for many years. The picture below appears to show a new-look cab on a 1957 7-tonner, with Bedford's own diesel engine.

*In 1974 Bedford plunged into the maximum weight "premium" end of the truck business. Eight TM models appeared that year in the 16 to 32-ton-gross bracket. This model pictured was a TM long-haul "concept" vehicle built to explore the possibilities of very advanced aero-dynamics and overall efficiency.*

*In 1977 Vauxhall received an order for £8 million worth of 6 cwt vans for the Post Office. At the time it was Vauxhall's biggest-ever single order. It is still supplying the Post Office as can be seen by this Combo LS van at the 1993 Motor Show.*

# Did You Know?

## Russian branch

A copy of a letter found in the company files dating from 1918 or 1920 had as a letter-head "Vauxhall Motors Ltd of Luton and St Petersburg." Subsequent inquiries revealed that Vauxhall had set up a sales branch in St Petersburg for importing motor cars, selling, servicing and warehousing spare parts. It transpires however that during the course of the Bolshevik Revolution the new branch was lost and never recovered.

## Postcards

In the 1930s a set of six postcards went on sale in a green envelope headed "3d Set of Six Postcard Photographs of The Vauxhall Works, Luton, Beds". Pictures were: Assembling Bedford Engines at the Vauxhall Factory, Machining Items for Gear Box Assembly at the Vauxhall factory, Part of Vauxhall's Sheet Metal Finishing Department, Vauxhall's Mammoth Canteen at Luton, Aerial view of the Vauxhall Factory and A Corner of Vauxhall's Press Shop and some of the mammoth presses. This set of six postcards now sells for £66!

## Women's work

Before the Second World War it was not Vauxhall policy to employ women in the production areas, as exclusively masculine shops were maintained as a definite plan. During the war it became necessary to employ women and they did a great job. A woman welfare supervisor was appointed to sort out such things as protective clothing, safety caps, shoes, clogs, "coupons", cloak-rooms, towels, soap, etc.

## Dunkirk effort

At the time of Dunkirk, Vauxhall night shift workers were on Whitsun holiday but were told to report for work that night. The workers returned and worked seven nights a week for the next three weeks doing 12-hour shifts. The machines never stopped.

## Waiting list

Before the Second World War Vauxhall needed men for the mass production line. In order to encourage workers they paid 30-50 per cent higher wages than other bigger engineering works and local hat factories. A waiting list was started which meant that potential workers had to wait for years to be taken on. It was not uncommon for employees living in north London to cycle to the Luton factory and back each day. When the war came conscription to the Armed Forces saw the waiting list reduce.

## Midnight music

The Vauxhall orchestra used to play in the main canteen frequently, not only during the three midday breaks but during the midnight break as well. In addition, in the 1940s Vauxhall was visited by many of the most famous artistes of the day: Evelyn Laye, Ethel Revnell, Gracie West, Pouishnoff, the BBC Theatre Orchestra with famous soloists – Vic Oliver, Elizabeth Welch, Gracie Fields, Charlie Kunz, Bennett and Williams, Patricia Rossborough, Tessie O'Shea, Carroll Gibbons.

### Meal poachers

A system of showing their passes before members were allowed in the canteen for lunch had to be brought in as a number of "strangers" were finding their way in for hot Vauxhall dinners! This meant that on occasions club members had to forfeit their meals as the amount of food was carefully rationed for the number of diners. There had even been instances of people coming from town to lunch at Vauxhall! (Vauxhall *Mirror*, January 1942).

### War dead

Twenty-three Vauxhall employees died in the First World War and 193 in World War Two. Plaques commemorating the dead of both world wars were taken down from the old canteen building which was demolished in 1991 and mounted a year later on a new monument built in a prominent position on the factory's Kimpton Road frontage.

### Summer break

In 1946 Vauxhall started shutting its factory for two weeks every summer, and as so much in Luton depended on Vauxhall, other parts of the town followed suit. Other employers were forced to copy Vauxhall and grant this holiday to their own work-force. Even the local schools adjusted the start of their school holidays accordingly.

### Fuel saver

In 1955 hanging tarpaulins and rubber sheets using warm air blowers and other devices were tried at the Vauxhall factory in Luton in order to cure the problem of lowered temperatures and draughts caused by the constant entrance and exit of vehicles through the great doors which were some 20 ft wide. The solution which was finally adopted was to create an air-lock tunnel with photo-electronically controlled doors at each end. It was estimated that this would save £6,000 a year in fuel costs (*Bedfordshire Magazine*, 1955).

### The magnet

The pull of Luton and Vauxhall Motors is affecting industries in Bedford, Watford and the new towns of Hemel Hempstead and Stevenage, states a spokesman of the Eastern Regional Board for Industry. So many men are leaving employment in the new towns for work in Luton that there is a danger of the towns becoming dormitory suburbs of Luton rather than the self-contained communities they were intended to be (*Bedfordshire Magazine*, 1957).

### Canada's choice

When the Viva was launched in 1963 it quickly became the best-selling British car in Canada, with the Victor in second place. The Vivas were sold in Canada under the names Epic and Envoy.

### Cold comfort

Local people used to say "When Vauxhall sneezes, Luton catches a cold". This was the time when Luton was dominated by vehicles and engineering. Luton has also been described as that "town next to Vauxhall".

### Inquiry

In the 1970s new GM investment went to Germany and Belgium rather than Luton. In the late 1980s Luton had real worries that GM might pull out altogether. Vauxhall had been a loss-maker for many years and truck producer Bedford was also in trouble. Alarmed about the way things were going, Luton Council set up a Motor Industry Inquiry and enlisted the help of Moss Evans, a former union leader, Sir Monty Finniston, retired British Steel Chief, and Chris Mayfield, the Bishop of Wolverhampton.

## The Equus

In 1978 the Equus (Latin for horse) "concept" sports car was shown publicly. The car represented the latest in sports car design and was the last all-British-designed Vauxhall. The car was tipped as a successor to the MGB as it was an affordable sports car for everyone. Plans were drawn up to have it made by Panther, on whose Lima sports car chassis the Equus was based. The car, however, was to remain a one-off styling exercise partly due to Vauxhall's design department being shut down in 1980 and transferred to Opel in Germany.

## Beauty bust-up

The 1980 Miss Vauxhall Beauty Contest turned into a violent shambles. The winner, Christine Pearson, was about to receive her crown when she was pushed in the back and off the platform. Watched by a crowd of 400, officials grappled with another contestant, who claimed the competition had been fixed. The chairman of the organizing committee, Dr Kenneth Pocock, said the panel of judges, which included the Vauxhall Chairman, and Luton Town FC Manager David Pleat, had been "entirely impartial and fair". Contestants had been given a few sherries before the contest to calm their nerves.

## Penny shock

In 1989 pensioner Vincent Cowell received a letter from Vauxhall stating his monthly pension was to go up from £48.18 to £48.19 - an increase of 1p. Upon further inquiry he was told the increase would be £1. A press office spokeswoman at Vauxhall said pension calculations were very complex and difficult to explain. "They depend on length of service, whether a lump-sum was taken and other factors." The spokeswoman confirmed that Mr Cowell would be getting £1 a month and explained

"There's a general decision pension rises of less than £1 will be made up to £1."

## Ton-up Nova

In 1990 during an RAC approved run the turbo-diesel Nova became Vauxhall's first car to do 100 miles to a gallon and top 100 mph. The £8,000 hatchback did 105 mpg at 32 mph then averaged 103 mph for an hour.

## Top dealer

A press advert in 1991 stated that Camden Motors in Lake Street, Leighton Buzzard, were the UK's number one volume dealers selling more new Vauxhalls than any other dealership group in the country.

## Fraud case

In 1991 investment fraudster Kevin Raisbeck was jailed for six years. His company, Bestdown Financial Services, handled investments for ex-Vauxhall workers. Some 65 clients lost over £1,300,000. Judge David Lowe said when passing sentence:

"In all your swindles you stole over £1 million in a deliberate bare-faced fraud and your calculated disregard for those unfortunate investors was to be compounded with your high life-style involving a Rolls-Royce, Bentleys, Porsches and a helicopter on which substantial amounts were used up. Your grandiose ideas, personal vanity and greed contributed to your criminal conduct."

## RSI award

A former Vauxhall machine operator was awarded £59,618 for suffering repetitive strain injury (RSI) at her job, in April 1992. Mrs Jane Inskip was awarded the sum for damage to her left thumb, in what was believed to be the highest court award involving RSI. Mrs Inskip developed osteoarthritis in her left thumb and parts of her hand when she loaded up to 500 gear wheels a day on to as many as seven finishing machines at the Luton plant for two years. The job involved turning, twisting and force, and the severe pains she suffered forced her to change to cleaning duties before she opted for voluntary redundancy in 1986.

## Quality

In 1993 Vauxhall Motors' Customer Assistance Centre became the first organization of its kind to gain registration to BS 5750 from the British Standards Quality Assurance. The following year BS 5750 Part Two was awarded to Vauxhall in recognition of the quality of its managements standards in the UK.

## Training

Guidelines Training Project, sponsored by the Department of Employment, was launched in 1993 at the Luton plant. The centre is open to all 4,500 employees in the Luton manufacturing plant and offers guidance and counselling. It identifies suitable courses available to employees with the aim of advancing their personal development at Vauxhall. More than 40 open-learning courses ranging from German to fibre optics are available.

## Heritage Centre

A superb collection of nearly 30 veteran, vintage and classic cars is housed in the Vauxhall Heritage Centre, opened in May 1993, which is situated behind the corporate headquarters in Luton. The centre is not a museum and not normally open to the general public. Many of the cars and commercial vehicles are used by Vauxhall and its dealer network for promotional work. The oldest car in the collection is a 1904 London-built 6 hp model with two seats and tiller steering. This car has completed virtually every London to Brighton run since 1950. Other vehicles in the collection include a 1911 Prince Henry, a D-type staff car from the First World War, a pair of 1923 tourers, a 1926 OE-type 30/98, and a 1929 six cylinder R-type.

## Ad aggro

In 1993 super-model Naomi Campbell's advert for the Spanish-built Corsa attracted criticism by a variety of anti-pornography and women's rights groups. The TV adverts showed five top models being upstaged by the Corsa. A Vauxhall spokeswoman said:

"Despite the fact that the Naomi Campbell ad was received very positively – we have had 30 or so concerns or complaints out of the 45 million people to see it – we will now show it after 9 pm. This move does not reflect pressure from advertising bodies or any campaign."

## Eating out

The *Black Horse* at Woburn was named Best Pub of 1994 in a survey by The Sunday Telegraph. The newspaper's critic, Tom Jaine, wrote that steak and oysters were a speciality, also "fresh tuna, sirloin in a marinade and lobster for the show-offs". Mr Jaine also wrote that the customer you are most likely to sit next to is an ex-Vauxhall worker.

## PM portrait

Former Vauxhall welder, Peter Deighan, who studied art at Luton College and earned £25 a week when he worked at Vauxhall in the 1960s, was commissioned to paint the first official portrait of the Prime Minister, John Major.

## Degree course

A university degree course has been specially created for the exclusive use of Vauxhall managers. Vauxhall are paying for the Business Systems Management degree at the University of Luton in what is a rare link between education and industry. Much of the teaching will take place at Vauxhall. Students will be taught about the law, health and safety, economic forecasting and the management of change, amongst other things.

### Recognition

Doing a stint overseas can be good for a GM executive's career. Vauxhall is not regarded as an easy ride and employees at Kimpton Road say that doing well at Vauxhall earns you a lot of gold stars from GM.

### HQ accolade

The design and landscaping of the Osborne Road headquarters won Vauxhall the Premier Award in the Greenspace competition, run by Bedfordshire County Council in 1991. The judges had special praise for the canteen where all the workers in the building, including the directors, eat. The canteen, where Princess Anne had lunch when she opened the building in 1990, has a sculptured layout and a continental feel, with murals depicting European resorts like Cannes.

### Welshman takes over

In 1996 Welshman Nick Reilly, 46, succeeded Charles Golden as Chairman and Managing Director of Vauxhall Motors. Mr Reilly joined General Motors in 1975 with the Detroit Diesel Allison Division in Wellingborough, Northamptonshire and gained international experience in Belgium three years later, before moving to General Motors in Detroit in 1979.

Mr Reilly was Manufacturing Director of Vauxhall's Astra and V6 engine plant at Ellesmere Port from 1990 to 1993. He then moved to become Vice-President of Quality and Reliability from 1993 until March 1996 for General Motors Europe in Zurich.

# Index